ALPHONSUS
EMPEROR OF GERMANY

REPRINTED IN FACSIMILE
FROM THE EDITION OF 1654

WITH AN INTRODUCTION AND NOTES
BY
HERBERT F. SCHWARZ

WILDSIDE PRESS

Copyright, 1913
BY
HERBERT F. SCHWARZ

The Knickerbocker Press, New York

PREFACE

THE text of this edition of *Alphonsus, Emperor of Germany*, is a reproduction in facsimile of a copy of the original edition designated British Museum copy 644 d. 50.

In the introduction no attempt has been made to solve the vexed questions of authorship and of date—questions that have been so ably discussed by others—but the endeavor has been to bring the play into relation with certain tendencies of the Elizabethan and Jacobean age.

In the notes appended to the volume the purpose has been to draw as largely as possible upon the records of contemporary travellers for the elucidation of the references made by the dramatist to conditions characteristic of the Germany of his day. To the praiseworthy pioneer work of Elze and to the scholarly investigations of Professor Parrott any one who attempts to bring out this play must necessarily be under special obligations. For the quotations frequently made from the edition of the former and for the guidance that the edition of the latter has been in connection with the comments on the text the writer wishes to express his deep indebtedness. The writer takes this opportunity, too, of recording his warm appreciation of the help which certain suggestions, made by his wife, have been to him.

Preface

The eminently satisfactory text that Professor Parrott has prepared in his collected plays of Chapman must render the attempt by another to further reconstruct the play a futile task. The present edition contains, therefore, only a very few text emendations, and these have been necessarily relegated to the notes.

H. F. S.

December 1, 1912.

INTRODUCTION

IN his *Literary Relations of England and Germany in the Sixteenth Century*, Herford makes the statement (p. 171) that "the score or so of early plays which profess to be founded on German history treat it with an open contempt much beyond what is demanded by the exclusive pursuit of scenic effect. Historic truth is not subordinated to dramatic truth but simply ignored." After characterising *Alphonsus of Germany* as "a crude and sanguinary travesty of an imperial election dispute in which the chief interest attaches to a wholly mythical love affair," he goes on to say that "the play is nevertheless probably the least unhistorical of the whole group."

The plot evolves out of the contention of Alphonso X of Castile and Richard, Earl of Cornwall, aspirants, during the *Interregnum* of the thirteenth century, to the crown of the Holy Roman Empire. The *dramatis personæ* include a large number of historic figures, but the plot and the interpretation of character are for the most part at variance with the record of history. Alphonsus, who in the play is depicted as a monster of iniquity, was an inoffensive monarch who never entered the land over which the dramatist would have us believe he established so bloody a rule. The partisan alignment credited to the different Electors does scant justice to the stand they actually took. Prince Edward (later Edward I of England) never placed foot upon the soil of Germany and thus escaped the charms of the German maiden to which in the play he succumbs so completely. Both the lives and the deaths of the principal characters were, in short, radically different from what a reading of the drama would lead one to suppose.

As an offset to the liberties which he takes with the events of history, the dramatist preserves, with rather exceptional fidelity, social customs and political institutions peculiar to the Empire.

If the play fails to render accurately the spirit of the age in which the action is laid, it indicates, though in an exaggerated manner, the violence and the trickery of the period in which it was written. Although it would be a libel to assert, without some modification, that the play taken as an entity illustrates the temper of those times, several incidents of brutality and craft that find place in it have their parallels, more or less close, in the history of the day. To attempt to identify the events or allusions in this drama with any one of these parallels would be hazardous, and yet, after a review of the evidence, the conclusion seems legitimate that the violence and intrigue of the Elizabethan age find their magnified reflection in *Alphonsus of Germany* and in dramas of that type. To the substantiation of this contention this brief introduction is devoted.

The first five maxims which Lorenzo impresses upon his willing pupil (see pp. 3–5 of the play) are, as Meyer has pointed out in *Machiavelli and the Elizabethan Drama*, more or less close renditions of precepts contained in Gentillet's *Discours sur les Moyens de bien gouverner. . . . Contre Nicholas Machiavel*. Of the sixth maxim:

> "Be alwaies jealous of him that knows your secrets,
> And therefore it behooves you credit few;
> And when you grow into the least suspect,
> With silent cunning must you cut them off,"

Introduction

Meyer (*Machiavelli and the Elizabethan Drama*, p. 136) says: "This is not to be found exactly as stated either in Machiavelli or Gentillet, but must have been perverted by the dramatists from *Principe*, 23." The last two lines of the sixth maxim are deserving of special attention. The murder of an accomplice or of one cognisant of some secret the betrayal of which would be costly, is not infrequent in the Elizabethan drama. What is worthy of emphasis is that it was apparently not exceptional in the history of that age. For instance, some of those who had a hand in the assassination of Darnley had to be rendered safe, to prevent their making revelations implicating others. One of them who wandered about in the dark, professing his guilt, was seized and thrust into prison. Another, from whom betrayal was feared, was knocked over the head and buried out of the way (Froude, *History of England from the Fall of Wolsey to the Defeat of the Spanish Armada*, vol. xi, p. 42). According to Weldon (*Court and Character of James I*, p. 23) when Sir Gervase Elwaies, Lieutenant of the Tower, learned of the design of Weston against the life of Overbury, he attempted, and at the time succeeded in, dissuading him from so foul a deed by stating among other things that "so many personages of honour would never cabinet such a secret in his breast, that might ruin them," thereby making Weston sensible of the dangers he ran. It was no uncommon thing in those days, "the game being bagged," as Lord Castlemaine expresses it, "to hang the spaniel which caught it, that its master might not appear."

Having delivered himself of the sixth maxim above quoted, Lorenzo, to teach his pupil by example, relates how he sent Julio Lentulus to his grave with a poison that the latter had entrusted to him. The particular virtue of this poison is that "it is twenty days before it works." Lorenzo has another poison, which "kills suddenly," and it is this poison which Alphonsus, who has profited by the nefarious teachings of his secretary, uses in killing the latter. In Act III, Alphonsus, after having drunk to the King of Bohemia, puts poison into the beaker. Bohemia, unaware of the treachery of the Emperor, drinks the poisoned draft. Later there is allusion to the fact that "in twenty hours" this poison will not work, a statement which has prompted Elze, somewhat arbitrarily, to identify it with the poison that Lorenzo had in his possession and to change the reading of the line in Act I from "twenty days" to "twenty hours." But slow-working poisons, as well as those that "killed suddenly," are referred to in the Elizabethan age. In 1579, for instance, there appeared before Don Bernardino in London a youth who claimed that he had a poison which, if applied to the lining of a man's hat, would dry up his brain and cause his death in *ten* days. He was ready, if the Ambassador approved, to try its power on the Prince of Orange. Although Don Bernardino had no great faith in the successful issue of the attempt, he nevertheless gave the youth his blessing and sent him on his evil mission (Froude, *History of England from the Fall of Wolsey to the Defeat of the Spanish Armada*, vol. xi, p. 590). The efficacy of this method of poisoning may be doubted. And yet it is in order to point out that in *The White Devil* (Act V, sc. 2) Lodovico sprinkles Brachiano's beaver with a poison, and Brachiano in the next scene, feeling the effects of the poison, exclaims:

"O, my brain's on fire!
The helmet is poisoned."

Introduction

In this play, moreover, allusion is made (Act V, sc. 1) to a poisoning attempt of the time. The lines,

> "To have poisoned . . .
> The pummel of his saddle . . . ,"

Reed points out, recall the case of Edward Squire, who in 1598 "was convicted of anointing the pummel of the Queen's saddle with poison, for which he was afterwards executed."

The notion of poisoning saddles seems to have been harboured, however, by others besides Squire. More than ten years earlier, in January, 1587, Stafford, a brother of Sir Edward, the Ambassador at Paris, came to Walsingham with the story that there was a conspiracy to take the life of the Queen, in which M. Chasteauneuf was the prime mover. According to Stafford's report Chasteauneuf had asked him whether he knew any one who, for a suitable reward, would undertake to kill Elizabeth. The Pope was ready to pay an annuity of ten thousand crowns to the successful assassin. Stafford further told Walsingham that he was approached by Destrappes, Chasteauneuf's secretary, to the same purpose. To ingratiate himself with them and thus to gather further details of the conspiracy, Stafford, according to his account, replied that there was a man named Moody, under arrest for debt at Newgate, who, he thought, might be prevailed upon. Destrappes expressing a readiness to interview Moody, he and Stafford went to the prison. There, according to Stafford, Moody proposed that if he were released (a thing that could be readily accomplished, for his debt was but a trifling one), he would either *poison the Queen's saddle* or introduce a bag of powder under her bed (Froude, *History of England from the Fall of Wolsey to the Destruction of the Spanish Armada*, vol. xii, pp. 336–337).

Chimerical as this proposal appears, the drama contains instances equally fantastic. Barabas in the *Jew of Malta* (Act IV, sc. 4) administers poison through a flower, which he presents to his victim to smell—a device which is employed in the French ballad entitled "La Marquise" (Bladé, *Poésies Populaires en Langue Française*, p. 26):

> "La reinne lui donne un bouquet
> Fait de fleurs tant jolies;
> Mais en flairant ce beau bouquet,
> Elle a perdu la vie."

In Marlowe's *Massacre at Paris*, sc. 2, Guise, addressing an apothecary, says:

> "Where are those perfumed gloves which late I sent
> To be poisoned?"

Guise, having come into possession of the gloves, sends them to the Queen. In the very words used in the play the Bishop of Rodez refers to this incident in his *History of Henry IV*. "Some historians," he states, "say that she was poisoned with a pair of *perfumed gloves;* but if I be not deceived, this is a falsity."

When Ithamore in Act II, sc. 3, of *The Jew of Malta* takes for granted that the letter which Barabas hands him is poisoned, he may well be alluding to a practice of the day. Certain it is that in an age not very distant, as time goes, the attempt of conveying poison on the paper of a letter was sometimes made. Witness the following incidents:—At Rome there was held in captivity by Pope Innocent VIII an unfortunate Turkish prince named Djem, whose existence was a menace to the rule of Bajazet, his brother. Living in constant fear of his life, Djem took the precaution on one occasion, in giving audience to an ambassador sent by his hostile-minded brother, of having that emissary

Introduction

lick every part of a letter he bore, both inside and out, before Djem would venture to so much as take it in his fingers (Fyvie, *Story of the Borgias*, pp. 27-28). The suspicion that was harboured by Djem proved to be ill-founded, but an instance occurred not many years later which proves the wisdom of the men who in crafty Italy were on their guard. Tomasino, a musician in the service of Alexander VI, undertook to bear to the Pope certain letters purporting to come from the community of Forli, of which Tomasino was a native. These letters Tomasino had contrived to envenom with a deadly poison. Possibly as a precaution against infection he therefore brought them rolled up within a hollow cane (Gordon, *Lives of Alexander VI and Cæsar Borgia*, p. 141). The carrying of letters in a cane was not unknown to the Elizabethan age and the bearer of poisoned letters would, therefore, have run no greater risk of infection then than in the time of the Borgias. This secret conveyance is alluded to in *Tancred and Gismunda*, as well as in Boccaccio's first novel of the fourth day, on which *Tancred and Gismunda* is based, but it played a part, too, in the history of the period. Froude records (*History of England from the Fall of Wolsey to the Defeat of the Spanish Armada*, vol. x, p. 297) that a lad was detected bringing secret letters to Mary Stuart "concealed in a staff."

The "toy," mentioned in Act I of *Alphonsus of Germany*, "to cast a man asleep" even when merely "smelt unto," though not a deadly poison, suggests one or two of the poisoning devices described above.

To the poisoned weapon there is no reference in *Alphonsus of Germany* and yet its use in the Elizabethan age and the allusions that are made to it in other dramas may serve as excuse for a paragraph or two regarding it. In Act V, sc. 1, of *Tamburlaine* occurs the line, "And every bullet dipt in poisoned drugs." In *The Devil's Charter*, Baglioni, exulting over the fallen Rotsi, exclaims, "You never drempt of a poysoned bullet, did you?" If one seeks for confirmation in the history of the period of this method of making assassination doubly sure, the death of the Prince of Orange is a case in point. Balthazar Gérard fired three poisoned balls into the body of the Protestant Prince (Morley, *Rise of the Dutch Republic*, p. 718).

Allusions to poisoned swords, rapiers, and daggers are frequent in the Elizabethan drama. To mention only a few:—In Act I, sc. 1, of *A Fair Quarrel*, Russell says,

"And I must tell you, sir, you have spoke swords,
And 'gainst the law of arms, poisoned the blades."

In *The Tragical History of Dr. Faustus*, sc. 6, occurs the phrase "envenomed steel." The surgeon called in to examine the King's wounds (*The Massacre at Paris*, sc. 24) exclaims,

"Alas, my lord, the wound is dangerous
For you are stricken with a poisoned knife."

But perhaps the most convincing example of an allusion to this contemporary practice is to be found in *Hamlet*. Whether or not the Hamlet-Laertes fencing bout found place in the *Ur-Hamlet*—in all probability Kyd's— there is certainly neither in Saxo Grammaticus nor in the *Hystorie of Hamblet*, based on Belleforest and published in 1608, a situation, however embryonic, which suggests this contest, much less the poisoning of the foils that are used in it. It was probably not merely the scenic limitations or the more noble conception of Hamlet's character that prompted Shakespeare, or the playwright responsible for the earlier drama, to

Introduction

replace the holocaust of the non-dramatic versions of the story by a new *dénouement*. It seems probable that the substitution was recognised as adding *vraisemblance* by association with a practice familiar to the age.

There was certainly one conspicuous case, antedating Shakespeare's *Hamlet* and involving the destinies of the nation, in which the poisoned rapier played its part. At the examination and voluntary confession of Edmond Yorke, taken the 20th of August, 1594, before Sir Michael Blount, Knt., Sir Edward Coke, Knt., etc. (Jardine, *Criminal Trials*, vol. ii, p. 271), it was elicited that at a certain conference there had been discussed "divers devices how to kill her majesty. Some spake of a little cross-bow of steel, that should carry a little arrow level a great way; and if the same did with a small arrow draw blood, being poisoned, she should not escape it. And this examinate was persuaded to have a little dagger, and so to kill her as she walked in the garden. But it was thought better to execute it with a rapier poisoned in the point, which is least suspected." Years later it was rumoured that Elizabeth's successor had been done to death by similar means. On Saturday, March 22d, five months after the discovery of the Gunpowder Plot, it is recorded (Stow's *Annales of King James*, p. 881) that a report was circulated, and continued to grow, to the effect that the King had been murdered. "Most reports agreed," the account adds, "that the king was stabd with an envenomed knife."

The drinking of poisoned wine, through a draught of which Bohemia is done to death in *Alphonsus of Germany*, was a common mode of assassination in the Elizabethan as in other ages, and is alluded to in the dramas of the period. Occasionally in the plays men meet their death accidentally, as it was at one time believed Pope Alexander VI met his, by drinking a poisoned beverage intended for another. Thus in *Women Beware of Women* the Duke drinks the poisoned cup which Bianca had prepared for his brother, the Cardinal. In *Hamlet* the Queen-mother swallows the potion which the King had set aside for her son.

The proffering of poisoned wine under a semblance of good will, a circumstance that adds to the dramatic effectiveness of the scene in *Alphonsus of Germany*, had its parallels, too, in history. Froude records (*History of England from the Fall of Wolsey to the Defeat of the Spanish Armada*, vol. i, p. 50) that "as a first evidence of returning cordiality, a present of wine was sent to Shan O'Neil from Dublin. It was consumed at his table, but the poison had been unskilfully prepared. It brought him and half his household to the edge of death, but no one actually died."

"Half this I drink unto your Highness health,
It is the first since we were joynd in Office,"

says Alphonsus to his victim before handing him the beaker he has just surreptitiously poisoned, reminding one of the words Piero gives expression to (*Antonio's Revenge*, Act I, sc. 1) when referring to the poisoned draught intended for Andrugio:

"That I should drop strong poison in the bowl,
Which I myself caroused unto his health
And future fortune of our unity!"

The introduction of poisoned drinks as a material part of the plot or allusions to them occur in a number of plays, of which a few only need be mentioned:—*Devil's Charter, Hoffman, Robert Earl of Huntington, The Bloody Banquet,* Webster's *Appius and Virginia, Thomas Wyatt, Sophonisba,* etc.

Introduction

Perhaps nothing so conclusively proves the prevalence of poisoning during the era and the decades preceding and following it than the ready attribution to its agency of illnesses of mysterious origin. When Don John of Austria died in 1578 of a sudden illness, some maintained that he had been poisoned either by Philip, or by the States, or by an assassin in the employ of Walsingham, while others were of the opinion that he died from breakdown occasioned by anxiety and his brother's suspicions (Froude, *History of England from the Fall of Wolsey to the Defeat of the Spanish Armada*, vol. xi, p. 158). It was uncertain whether poison or natural illness caused the death of the Earl of Mar (Froude, vol. x, p. 448). Queen Elizabeth took the precaution after Mary had thrown herself on her bounty to direct that the food consumed by the Queen of Scots should be prepared by her own servants, "lest an accidental illness should be imputed to poison" (Froude, vol. ix, p. 240). And Mary profited by the dominant suspicion of the age in seeking release. Froude states (vol. ix, p. 457) that she wrote to La Mothe Fénelon to present a sharp demand for her liberation, on the ground that she was "seized with symptoms of the same disorder which had so nearly killed her at Jedburgh. They were harmless, being the result merely of pills, but she had calculated justly on the alarm of the Queen of England, who dreaded nothing so much as any serious illness of her prisoner which the world would attribute to poison." The Bishop of Rodez records (*History of Henry IV*) that when Charles IX fell mortally sick, he was believed by many to have been poisoned, and that when Henry III was stricken with an ear affliction, he attributed his malady to poison, accusing Monsieur. Aiken makes the statement (*Memoirs of the Court of James I*, vol. i,

p. 341) that after a time it became the belief, "not merely of the vulgar, or of a party, but of persons of the highest rank and consequence," that Prince Henry was poisoned by Viscount Rochester. "Nor did the king himself escape the horrid and incredible charge of being privy to the poisoning of his son, at least after the fact." Alphonsus' audacity in accusing those of a rank all but equal to his own of being poisoners must have seemed plausible to an audience of the Elizabethan age when poisoning was a practice resorted to in a most conscienceless manner. Marvell several decades later was thought to have died of poison and Birrell points out (*Life of Marvell*) that "such a suspicion in those bad times was not far-fetched."

In Act II of *Alphonsus of Germany* two peasants are prompted to make an attempt upon the life of Richard through an anonymous letter. Crude as is this device, it is only one of many instances in the Elizabethan drama of the use of the letter for treacherous purposes, and for at least some of these instances there are historic parallels. In Fletcher's *Bonduca*, Act III, sc. 2, the daughter of Bonduca sends a letter to Junius protesting her love for him and arranging for a *rendez-vous*. She closes her epistle with "the gods, my Junius, keep thee, and me to serve thee!" Junius has every need of the gods' assistance, for the faithless maiden soon shows him what sort of service he may expect from her. Arrived at the trysting-place with his friends, he is apprehended, called a salt-itch'd slave, and threatened with death, from which, however, he is spared by the intervention of Caratach. Francisco de Medicis in *The White Devil* is even more cunning in inditing an amorous epistle that he hopes, and not vainly, will work mischief. He gives instructions to his servant to deliver to Vittoria a letter offering his love, at such time

Introduction xvii

when the followers of Brachiano, her lover, may be near to intercept it or demand the nature of its contents.

Instances of the use of forged letters to calumniate the innocent are found in Middleton. Geraldine in *The Family of Love*, hoping to involve in trouble the guardian of the girl he loves, presents a letter to the guardian's wife. This letter, purporting to come from a woman in the country, relates how the guardian has gotten her with child. In *More Dissemblers Besides Women*, Lactantio, at the instigation of the Duchess, draws up a letter in the General's handwriting and affixes to it the General's signature. The letter contains a dishonourable proposal of love and the Duchess hopes, through its instrumentality, to have the General arrested. She has, however, a subtler reason for desiring his arrest than Lactantio supposes. Secure in her power, she confronts the General with the forged letter and offers him a love which she pretends he has solicited. In *Phœnix*, Act V, sc. 1, occurs the line, " 'T is forg'd against mine honour and my life."

A somewhat different use of the letter is made in Massinger's *Duke of Milan*. In this play Francisco, to undermine the constancy of Marcelia and thus accomplish his designs upon her honour, gives her a letter written by her husband, Lodovico Sforza, which, without an explanation of the circumstances under which it was written and of the contingency under which its instructions were to be carried out, gives the false impression that the Duke, instead of loving his wife with an extravagant passion, really has a deep hatred for her.

Interesting examples of the letter forged for treacherous purposes occur in Fletcher's *Valentinian* and in *The Knight of Malta*. In the former play Maximus, in order to remove every obstacle that threatens the accomplishment of his vengeance, resolves to clear from his path the too faithful Aëcius whose loyalty to the tyrannical Valentinian is unswerving. He accordingly draws up a letter and places it where Valentinian cannot fail to come upon it. In the letter Maximus is urged to keep a vigilant eye upon Aëcius, whose popularity among the soldiers, it is alleged, is so great that they are on the point of dethroning the Emperor and raising Aëcius to the pinnacle of the State in Valentinian's stead. The credulous Valentinian hereupon resolves to have Aëcius killed. In *The Knight of Malta*, Zanthia, the mistress of Mountferrat, forges a letter of a treasonable purport and attaches to it the signature of Oriana, who is guiltless of conspiring with the Turkish enemy and, contrary to the impression which the letter conveys, is equally guiltless of entertaining love for him.

The instances of the use of the treacherous letter in Fletcher—their number might be added to—deserve some emphasis, for Fletcher's father played an important rôle in the life, or perhaps more accurately in the death, of Mary Stuart, a woman against whom, many believe, was directed a forgery of the most daring magnitude. It was Fletcher's father who as chaplain was a witness to Mary's tragic end at Fotheringay and who, when the axe had fallen on her head, pronounced, amid the silence of the awe-struck assemblage, the solemn words: "So perish all the Queen's enemies."

Circumstances of the career of Mary Queen of Scots must have frequently been described to the family circle by one who had been present in an official capacity at her spectacular execution and mention must have been made more than once of the famous "casket letters." If this assumption is sound, it may account for Fletcher's partiality for the forged letter written to calumniate, or bring about the ruin of, the innocent. Even if Fletcher placed no faith in the contention that the "casket letters" were forged, the attribution of their origin to forgery must have appealed strongly to his sense of the dramatic. The "casket letters," it will be recalled, were letters and sonnets discovered in an old casket. They were neither signed nor directed, but they were declared, after comparison with Mary Stuart's letters, to have been written by her and to have been sent to Bothwell. Their character, if genuine, tells heavily against Mary's innocence.

The contention that the treacherous letter as used in the Elizabethan drama has an historic complexion does not rest, however, on the authenticity or lack of authenticity of the "casket letters." Many citations might be made from the history of the period to confirm the impression that the forged letter was frequently employed to embarrass and cast suspicion upon its alleged inditers. Essex, on trial, asserted that letters counterfeited in his name had been sent into Ireland to Sir Christopher Blunt, the hope of the writers being to cast reflection on his honour and his reputation. He furthermore testified that one Bales had confessed that he had been compelled to forge Essex's handwriting in at least a dozen letters. The Attorney-General by way of reply contended that Bales had been hired thereunto by John Daniels, one of Essex's own men, to the end that if Essex's own handwriting were submitted as evidence against him, he might deny its authenticity (Jardine, *Criminal Trials*, vol. i, p. 328).

Gerard is authority for the statement that it was an "inveterate habit" of conspirators at that period to drop compromising documents in places where their discovery was assured. He instances (*What was the Gunpowder Plot?*, p. 218) the placing of a letter in the court of Salisbury House, which letter purported to come from five Catholics. Although professing to be appalled and horrified by the Gunpowder Plot, these men are represented as warning Cecil that they have pledged themselves to assassinate him if he makes the occasion the excuse for relentless activity against the Catholics. The letter was in all probability a forgery, maliciously framed against the Catholics. The resourcefulness of Throgmorton also bears testimony to the prevalence of forgery for defamatory purposes. Before he was carried off under arrest, Throgmorton found time to write a few hasty words in cipher to Mendoza. He said that he had denied all knowledge of certain compromising papers and had explained that they must have been left in his house by some one who desired to do him injury (Froude, *History of England from the Fall of Wolsey to the Defeat of the Spanish Armada*, vol. xi, pp. 642–643).

Welwood is of the opinion that Cecil was aware of the Gunpowder Plot long before its discovery, and that the famous letter to Monteagle, presumably coming from one of the conspirators, was "a contrivance of his own." Jardine thinks it not at all unlikely that the letter was, as Osborn calls it, a "neat device" which the Secretary adopted to prevent the real mode of the discovery from becoming known (Jardine, *Criminal Trials*, vol. ii, p. 189). The hypothesis that Tresham (the brother-in-law of Monteagle), or Monteagle acting on information received from him, laid bare the conspiracy before the government, thus enabling it to frame the letter of warning, has its defenders. This was the theory held by Greenway, one of the Jesuits who was accused of being a party to the plot (Hume-Stafford, *History of England*, vol. i, p. 685).

In 1586, in order that more light might be shed on

Introduction   xxi

the Babington conspiracy, the Queen suggested that a ciphered letter be conveyed to Ballard as if from one of the confederates. It was hoped that thereby Ballard might be lured into writing an answer. But Phillips, a professional decipherer, was unable to furnish a key and hence the project had to be abandoned (Froude, *History of England from the Fall of Wolsey to the Defeat of the Spanish Armada*, vol. xii, p. 272). The name of Phillips turns up later on again. The bearer of it had fallen under suspicion because of a correspondence with Hugh Owen. Accordingly another agent, named Barnes, was employed by Cecil to write a letter purporting to come from Phillips, who was then in England, and carry it to Owen, who was sojourning in Flanders. This plan miscarried owing to the arrest of Barnes in Dover (Gerard, *What was the Gunpowder Plot?*, pp. 111–112).

The forging of one side of a correspondence, though it might sometimes tempt the innocent into the commission of treasons for which they had previously had only a mild sympathy, served the prime purpose of trapping the guilty into an admission of their guilt. More subversive of justice was the attempt to force Gowrie into confession. He was induced, notwithstanding his protest that such a statement would be an untruth, to profess in a letter to the King that he had been involved in several conspiracies against his Majesty which he could reveal in a private interview. Those who counselled him to take this step urged that the letter, being of a general character, would pique the King's curiosity, and that at the audience which was certain to be granted him as a consequence, he could explain that the letter was only an expedient to enable him to secure the attention of the King for the stating of his own case. Threatened with death if he did not comply with the suggestion, he yielded. Arran pledged his sacred word of honour that he should be safe. But at the trial, where nothing was proved against Gowrie, the letter was produced and resulted in his conviction (Andrew Lang, *James VI and the Gowrie Mystery*, p. 120). A similar case is recorded in Gordon's *Lives of Pope Alexander VI and his Son Cæsar Borgia* (p. 119). The Pope, being anxious to propitiate the Castilian monarchs and their ally, Frederick, King of Naples, denied having granted a certain dispensation which had incensed them, alleging that it was forged by the secretary of the briefs, one Monseigneur Florida, Archbishop of Cosenza. The unfortunate scapegoat was put under arrest. The Pope commissioned a scamp named Giovanni Merades to visit Florida and under pretence of playing chess with him to persuade him, innocent as he was, to acknowledge himself guilty. As an inducement Florida was promised reinstatement in the Pope's good graces, the restoration of all the benefices of which he had been deprived, and even promotion to greater dignities than he had ever enjoyed. On the strength of the confession which the deluded Archbishop was thus inveigled into making, his estate was confiscated and given to Borgia.

The following testimony of Cobham is cited not necessarily for its authenticity, for Cobham was given to contradiction, but in substantiation of the tendency to forgery at that period. In denying that he had made a declaration attributed to him incriminating Raleigh, Cobham said: "That villain Wade [the Lieutenant of the Tower] did often solicit me, and, not prevailing, got me, by a trick, to write my name on a piece of white paper, which I, thinking nothing, did; so that if any charge came under my hand, it was forged by that villain Wade, by writing something above my hand, without my consent or knowledge" (Gerard, *What Was the Gunpowder Plot?*, pp. 202–3).

The section of this introduction that has to do with the forged letter may fittingly be closed with a brief allusion to forged letters patent. In Stow's *Annales* (p. 865) it is stated that "James Steward was executed for counterfeiting the King's hand, thinking thereby to have procured the Great Seale of England, unto a forged letters patents, for the passing and conveying of an hundred marks by the year, of Crown land unto himself." In Part II. of Heywood's *Edward IV* a stage direction reads, "Enter Rufford and Fogge with the counterfait letter-patents. Shore stands aside." This conversation then ensues:

Rufford: This is King Richard's hand, I know it well,
   And this of thine is justly counterfeit,
   As he himself would swear it were his own.
Shore: The King's hand counterfeit? List more of that.
Rufford: Why every letter, every little dash
   In all respects alike. Now may I use
   My transportation of my corn and hides,
   Without the danger of forbidding law.

When the Empress bids Alphonsus (p. 41) to cut off her nose, she is alluding to a barbarous punishment of the age, which is mentioned in not a few dramas. In *Blurt Master Constable*, Act II, sc. 2, Imperia says, "Trivia, strip that villain; Simperina, pinch him, slit his wide nose." Isabella in *The White Devil* in her eagerness to do physical violence to Vittoria, who has supplanted her in her husband's affections, proposes among other things to "cut off her nose." Jane Shore in Part II of *Edward IV* is fearful of being led before the offended Queen lest the latter "slit her nose" or "spurn her unto death." In Middleton's *Anything for a Quiet Life*, Knavesby proposes to go home and cut his "wife's nose off." Aiken records (*Memoirs of the Court of James I*, vol. i, pp. 189-190) that Jonson, Marston, and Chapman were in danger of having their ears and noses slit upon complaint of Sir James Murray, gentleman of the bedchamber, who took offence at their lines regarding the Scots in their joint play *Eastward Ho*.

The ear, however, more often than the nose suffered mutilation. The offences for which these punishments were imposed were frequently of a trivial character. In 1559, a dishonest purveyor who had taken smelts for the queen's provision and had then sold them at an advanced price was as a punishment placed for three days in the pillory in Cheapside, with a "bawdricke of smelts" about his neck, and upon his forehead a paper indicating his offence. As a culmination to these indignities he was to have lost one of his ears, but owing to the petition of the Lord Mayor, he was instead condemned to a prolonged imprisonment (Hayward, *Annals of the First Four Years of Elizabeth's Reign*, p. 30). Thomas Pound, a Lancashire gentleman, upon whom had been imposed a fine for infringement of the laws against Catholics, under Elizabeth, was a victim of the bigotry from which the reign of her successor was not free. Pound had ventured to send a petition to the King on behalf of one Skitel, a neighbour of his, who had been condemned to death for "harbouring a Jesuit." For his temerity Pound was sentenced to pay a fine of £1000 and to stand in the pillory at Westminster and Lancaster. It was further proposed that he should have an ear cut off at each of these places. Owing to the public indignation occa-

Introduction   xxv

sioned by this harsh sentence and the intercession of the Queen as well as that of the Spanish and the French ambassadors, the punishment was modified in the execution, and even Skitel's sentence of death was changed to one of banishment (Hume-Stafford, *History of England*, p. 684). The part of Pound's sentence which has to do with the loss of his ears is of pertinence in this connection. When both ears were to be forfeited, it seems to have been a not unusual custom to make the excision of one ear in a designated place and to lop off the other ear in a different locality. The following quotation from *The Blind Beggar of Bednall Green* is in keeping with the citation just made: "This reprieve is counterfeit and made by me, your ordinary pasport maker, that should have lost an ear at Salisbury, and another at Northampton."

There are not a few allusions in the drama of the period to the custom of amputating the ear. References to it may be found, to mention only a few instances, in Marston's *What You Will*, Marlowe's *Massacre at Paris*, Middleton's *Michaelmas Term* and *Anything for a Quiet Life*, Webster's *Appius and Virginia*, and in the Prologue of *The Woman Hater*. As Prof. Ashley H. Thorndike has pointed out (*The Influence of Beaumont and Fletcher on Shakspere*, p. 58), the allusion in the Prologue of *The Woman Hater* is reminiscent of the plight in which the collaborators of *Eastward Ho* found themselves. A wag who had written an abusive satire, concluded with these lines:

"Now God preserve the king, the queen, the peers,
And grant the author long may wear his ears,"

whereat his Majesty was much amused.

In the reign of Henry VIII able-bodied men found begging were, for a first offence, merely whipped. A second conviction was punished by the cropping of the offender's ears (Traill, *Social England*, vol. iii, p. 120). According to the Act of 1530–1 scholars of the universities, sailors, pardoners, and others were for the first offence whipped in the same manner as ordinary vagabonds; for the second, they were to be scourged two days, to be placed in the pillory, and were furthermore to forfeit one of their ears; for the third, they were to be scourged again, to suffer the humiliation of the pillory, and to lose their remaining ear (Traill, *Social England*, vol. iii, pp. 250–1).

An even more revolting spectacle is that conjured up by the threat to tear from the body the victim's heart. The second murderer (*Massacre at Paris*, sc. 21) exclaims, "O that his heart were leaping in my hand." Lines as sanguinary appear even in such a play as *A Woman Killed with Kindness:*

"Rip up my breast, and with my bleeding heart
Present him as a token."

Lodowick (*The Jew of Malta*, Act II, sc. 2) declares he will have Mathias's heart. The Cardinal in the *Blind Beggar of Bednall Green* voices this sentiment, so out of accord with his Christian office:

"O I could tear my flesh
And eat his heart for this disparagement,"

lines which remind one of the unnatural appetite of Nicke in *A Woman Killed with Kindness:*

"I cannot eate,
But had I Wendol's heart I would eate that."

Philip in *Lust's Dominion* threatens to "beat that dog to death that sounds retreat," and adds "I'll tear his

Introduction xxvii

heart out that dares name that sound." Citations of this character—and they might be multiplied—sound strange to the modern ear, but they probably did not shock the robust nerves of the Elizabethans. In fact, language no less violent was under extreme circumstances used at that time in civil life as well as on the stage. When Essex was accused of treason, he exclaimed, "This hand shall pull out this heart when any disloyal thought shall enter it" (Strickland's *Queen Elizabeth*). Lord Gray, one of the commissioners at the trial of Davison, who was made a scapegoat by Elizabeth for the execution of Mary Stuart, in delivering his judgment used these words, that "in revenge for his sovereign, he [Davison] would have been the first to have rent his heart out of his body" (Froude, *History of England from the Fall of Wolsey to the Destruction of the Spanish Armada*, vol. xii, p. 375).

This punishment was actually imposed, among others equally revolting, upon the assassin of William the Silent. It was decreed that his heart should be torn from his breast and flung in his face. The sentence was literally executed (Motley, *Rise of the Dutch Republic*, pp. 719–720), as inhuman a proceeding as that perpetrated by the Aztecs on their human sacrifices (Prescott's *Conquest of Mexico*, vol. i, p. 79).

Another execrable punishment was the chopping off of the hand of an offender. Allusions to it are not infrequent in the drama. In *The Royal King and Loyal Subject*, the Loyal Subject, commanded to send one of his daughters to court, says:

"Had the King commanded
One of my hands, I had sent it willingly;
But her! yet Kings must not be dallied with,"

which reminds one of the words used by Susan in *A Woman Killed with Kindness*,

"Will Charles
Have me cut off my hands and send them Acton?"

In Traill's *Social England* (vol. iii, p. 364) it is recorded that in the reign of Elizabeth the exportation of raw materials was sharply discouraged. The exportation of a live sheep might, in the case of a first offence, cost a man his hand.

The courage with which the victims bore their punishment—fine examples of the physical hardihood of that age of iron as well as of gold—blots out in some measure, or at any rate directs attention from, the appalling cruelty of the following incident. A Puritan lawyer, John Stubbs by name, wrote a pamphlet, wherein he commented rather too frankly and distastefully regarding the match at one time proposed between Elizabeth and Alençon (Creighton, *Queen Elizabeth*, p. 172). Both Stubbs and his book-seller, Page, were sentenced to lose their right hand. They were conducted from the Tower to a scaffold erected in front of the palace at Westminster, and "their right hands were struck off with a cleaver driven through the wrist with a beetle." While the dismembered stump was being cauterised with a hot iron, Page said proudly, "I have left there a true Englishman's hand." Stubbs, exhausted from the flow of blood, nevertheless waved his hat with all the energy he could muster and cried, "God save Queen Elizabeth," before dropping in a faint (Froude, *History of England from the Fall of Wolsey to the Destruction of the Spanish Armada*, vol. xi, p. 181).

Characterised by loyalty, though tempered some-

Introduction

what doubtless by self-interest, is an incident, not unlike in some respects the case just related, which occurred some decades earlier. Holinshed records that "on the 10th of June, 1541 Sir Edmund Knevet, knight, of Norfolk, was arraigned before the king's justices . . . for striking of one master Clere of Norfolk, servant with the Earl of Surrey, within the king's house in the tennis court. There was first chosen to go upon the said Edmund, a quest of gentlemen, and a quest of yeomen, to inquire of the said strife, by the which inquests he was found guilty, and had judgement to lose his right hand. . . . At the time when this sentence was to be executed, Sir Edmund Knevet desired that the king, of his benign grace, would pardon him of his right hand, and take the left, for (quoth he) if my right hand be spared, I may hereafter do such good service to his grace, as shall please him to appoint." So touched was the King by this plea that he granted Knevet a free pardon.

It may be in order at this point to make reference to the fact that in the Elizabethan age the hand was looked upon as a responsible agent and not only were blame and praise attached to it, but self-inflicted punishment was at times visited upon it for its failure to execute a difficult and desired task or for its activity in a cause that led to humiliating or other evil results. In *Alphonsus of Germany* (p. 67) Alexander gives his hand credit for murdering the Emperor:

"This happy hand, blest be my hand therefore,
Reveng'd my Fathers death upon his Soul."

More often, however, the hand is taken to task for some evil done or good left undone. In *Tamburlaine*, Part II, Act IV, sc. 3, for instance, Olympia, pretending that she has an ointment which will render the part of the body that is anointed with it invulnerable, persuades her importunate and lustful lover, Theridamas, to stab her neck. Theridamas in his credulity strikes the blow, and when he realises the consequence of his act exclaims:

"What have I slain her! Villain stab thyself;
Cut off this arm that murdered thy love."

When Cranmer, who had signed a recantation of Luther's doctrines, was led to the stake in 1556, he repented of his previous weakness and gave utterance to these memorable words, stamping him the hero that in life's supreme moment he showed himself to be: "Forasmuch as my hand offended, writing contrary to my heart, my hand shall first be punished therefor, for when I come to the fire, it shall first be burned!" When the fire was kindled and rose, he held his right hand steadfastly and immovably in the consuming flame so that all those present might see it burn away before his body was touched. Mucius is supposed to have had conferred upon him the surname of Scævola because after having mistakenly killed another, in the belief that it was Porsena, he is said to have burned off the hand that served him so ill. The incident is recorded in Plutarch and in Livy (de Beaufort, *l'Incertitude des cinq premiers siècles de l'histoire Romaine*). Scævola is a character in Heywood's *Rape of Lucrece* and his spoken lines:

"Oh too rash, Mutius, hast thou missed thy aime?
And thou base hand that didst direct my poniard
Against a peasants breast, behold thy error
Thus will I punish: I will give thee freely
Unto the fire, nor will I wear a limbe,
That with such rashnesse shall offend his Lord,"

Introduction xxxi

must have sounded like a distorted version of Cranmer's declaration.

Reference may at this point be made to a custom which seems to have its reflection in some of the plays of the day. After Mary Stuart's execution all of the objects spattered with her blood, including her beads, Paternoster, handkerchief, the cloth on the block, and the scaffold were burned, so that none of them might be taken away (Froude's *History of England from the Fall of Wolsey to the Destruction of the Spanish Armada*, vol. xii, p. 361). Just before her execution Mary, noticing that her chaplain and her ladies were not present, asked the reason of their absence. Kent told her he feared they might scream or faint or attempt perhaps *to dip their handkerchiefs in her blood.* The last assigned reason has an astonishingly close parallel in *The Spanish Tragedy.* Hieronimo, it will be recalled, dips a handkerchief in his son's blood and vows not to part with it till he has achieved his revenge. In Marlowe's *Dido* it is related that Pyrrhus took his father's flag "and dipped it in the old king's chill-cold blood."

The breaking on the wheel, referred to on p. 67 of *Alphonsus of Germany*, was a common punishment of the day. Allusions to it are found in *Tamburlaine*, Part II, in *Hoffman*, in *The White Devil*, in *The Duchess of Malfi*, etc. After the rising of the Castilians in Scotland and the murder of the captured regent, Lennox, Cawdor, who was taken, was broken on the wheel (Froude's *History of England from the Fall of Wolsey to the Destruction of the Spanish Armada*, vol. x, p. 285). The Bishop of Rodez, in his *History of Henry IV*, records that "the Baron of Fontanelles for having had a hand in the Byron conspiracy and besides that treating of his own accord with the Spaniards to deliver to them a little island on the coast of Britany, was broke on the wheel in the Greve by sentence of the Great Council." Coryat, one of the travellers of the age who has left an interesting record of his impressions and gleanings in foreign lands, states (*Crudities*, vol. ii, p. 308) that he "observed in a great many places, on both sides of the Rhene, more gallowes and wheeles betwixt Mentz and Colen, then ever I saw in so short a space in all my life, especially within a few miles of Colen." Coryat describes (*Crudities*, vol. i, p. 159) in some detail the method of execution by the wheel. Referring to a wheel he saw on his jaunt through France, he states that on it "the bodies of murderers only are tormented and broken in peeces with certaine yron instruments, wherewith they breake their armes first, then their legs and thighes, and after their breast: If they are favoured their breast is first broken. That blow on their breast is called the blow of mercy, because it doth quickly bereave them of their life. This torment of the wheele I find in Aristotle to have been used amongst the ancient Grecians also Who in the seventh booke of his Ethicks and third Chapter, useth the word τροχίξευς which signifieth to be tormented with the wheele." In Germany the penalty of being broken on the wheel was most frequently associated with the crime of murder. But in the Netherlands, according to Fynes Moryson, another traveller of the age, the punishment was also imposed upon counterfeiters (*Itinerary*, vol. iv, p. 471).

To the last-mentioned traveller one turns for elucidation of the strangely barbarous custom referred to on pp. 69–70 of *Alphonsus of Germany*. When the punishment to be meted out to Alexander is under discussion, Prince Edward says:

"I would adjudge the Villain to be hang'd
As here the Jewes are hang'd in *Germany*."

Introduction

To this the Elector of Saxony assents:

> "Young Prince it shall be so; go dragg the Slave
> Unto the place of execution:
> There let the *Judas*, on a Jewish Gallowes,
> Hang by the heels between two English Mastives,
> There feed on Doggs, let Doggs there feed on thee,
> And by all means prolong his miserie."

"Neare Lindaw," writes Fynes Moryson (*Itinerary*, vol. iv, p. 289), " I did see a malefactor hanging in Iron chaines on the gallowes, with a Mastive Dogge hanging on each side by the heeles, so as being starved, they might eate the flesh of the malefactor before himselfe died by famine. And at Franckford I did see the like spectacle of a Jew hanged alive in chaines, after the same manner." This method of execution, modified according to local custom or caprice, seems to have been practised at one time or another in diverse places. In the year 1399 one of those miraculous occurrences that are so characteristic of the credulity of the Middle Ages, and so strange a mingling of devotion and religious antipathy, was said to have taken place in Posen. Certain Jews of Posen were accused of having persuaded a poor woman to steal the Host for them. The sacred thing was, according to the account, taken to a cellar in the Ghetto, where the Jews showed their aversion for it by thrusting into it their knives. Then occurred the astonishing thing. The Host began to bleed and to perform miracles. In fear the Jews threw it into a swamp, but it still continued to perform miracles, thereby attracting the notice of the Christians. For this alleged desecration a punishment resembling closely the diabolical torment referred to above was imposed. The woman who had stolen the Host, the

Jewish Rabbi, and the most aged of the Jews were together with dogs attached to posts and were slowly roasted to death (Kohnt, *Geschichte der Deutschen Juden*, pp. 287–8). Discrimination against Jews not only in life but even in death is, furthermore, referred to by Alphonse Levy (*Geschichte der Juden in Sachsen*, p. 47). According to this author Jewish criminals, condemned to death in Leipzig, who failed to recant their belief, were not considered worthy to be hung upon a Christian gallows; wherefore a special gallows was assigned to them. If one may believe Roger Ascham, a form of execution not radically different from those described above was practised by the Turk, who, however, in the instance recorded, visited the punishment not on the unbelieving Jew but upon the Christian unbeliever.

In the foregoing sketch the writer pleads guilty to having every now and then strayed into a discussion of matters which, while legitimately classifiable under the headings of violence and intrigue, may at times have seemed to the reader to have only an indirect bearing on *Alphonsus of Germany*. But, if he has overstepped his prerogative, it has been in the hope of re-emphasising certain tendencies of the age which find exaggerated expression in this drama, and thus of smoothing the way for an understanding of certain incidents in the play that, without such an explanation, would seem grotesque and unnatural. A period of literature that cultivated the chronicle history play; that put on the stage dramatisations of contemporary events like the tragedies of *Byron* and *Sir John Van Olden Barnavelt;* that occasionally used the drama for the presentation of a political allegory, as in the case of Middleton's *Game at Chess;* and that in the field of the domestic tragedy was even known to draw for its subject-matter upon an actual murder case of the time; a period of literature that throws so much interesting light on customs and manners peculiar to the day and through which runs the strong current of late 16th and early 17th century life—did not, it may be safely concluded, fail to reflect in fulness the brutal practices and the subterranean methods that prevailed at the time.

THE
TRAGEDY
OF
ALPHONSUS
EMPEROUR
OF
GERMANY

As it hath been very often Acted (with
great applause) at the Privat house
in BLACKFRIERS by his late
MAIESTIES Servents.

By *George Chapman* Gent.

LONDON,
Printed for HUMPHREY MOSELEY, and are to be
sold at his Shopp at the Princes-Arms
in St. *Pauls* Church-yard 1654.

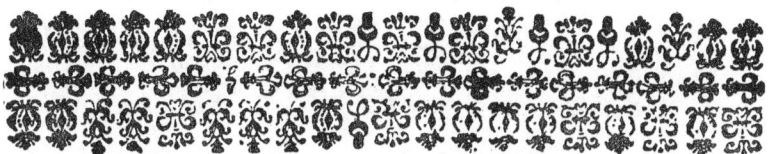

To the Reader

I Shall not need to bespeak thee Courteous, if thou hast seen this Piece presented with all the Elegance of Life and Action on the *Black-Friers* Stage; But if it be a Stranger to thee, give me leave to prepare thy acceptation, by telling thee, it was receiv'd with general applause, and thy judgement (I doubt not) will be satisfied in the reading.

I will not raise thy Expectation further, nor delay thy Entertainment by a tedious Preface. The Design is high, the Contrivement subtle, and will deserve thy grave Attention in the perusall.

Farewell.

Dramatis Personæ.

Alphonsus Emperour of *Germany*.
King of *Bohemia*.
Bishop of *Mentz*.
Bishop of *Collen*.
Bishop of *Tryer*.
Pallatine of the *Rhein*.
Duke of *Saxon*.
Marquess of *Brandenburgh*.
} The seven Electors of the *German* Empire.

Prince *Edward* of *England*.
Richard Duke of *Cornwall*.
Lorenzo de Cipres, Secretary to the Emperour.
Alexander his Son, the Emperours Page.
Isabella the Empress.
Hedewick Daughter to the Duke of *Saxon*.
Captain of the Guard.
Souldiers.
Jaylor.
Two Boores.

ALPHONSUS
Emperour of *Germany*.

Enter Alphonsus *the Emperour in his night-gown, and his shirt, and a torch in his hand,* Alexander de Tripes *his Page, following him.*

Al. Boy, give me the Master Key of all the doors.
To Bed again, and leave me to my self. [*Exit*
Is *Richard* come? have four Electors [*Alexder.*
sworn
To make him Keisar in despite of me?
Why then *Alphonsus* it is time to wake.
No Englishman, thou art too hot at hand,
Too shallow braind to undermine my throne;
The Spanish Sun hath purifi'd my wit,
And dry'd up all gross humours in my head,
That I am sighted as the King of Birds,
And can discern thy deepest Stratagems.
I am the lawful German Emperour,
Chosen, enstall'd, by general consent;
And they may tearm me Tyrant as they please,
I will be King, and Tyrant if I please;
For what is Empire but a Tyrannie?
And none but children use it otherwise.
Of seven Electors, four are falln away,
The other three I dare not greatly trust;
My Wife is Sister to mine enemy,
And therefore wisely to be dealt withall;
But why do I except in special,
When this position must be general,

B   That

That no man living must be credited,
Further than tends unto thy proper good.
But to the purpose of my silent walk;
Within this Chamber lyes my Secretary,
Lorenzo de Cipres, in whose learned brain
Is all the compass of the world contain'd;
And as the ignorant and simple age
Of our forefathers, blinded in their zeal,
Receiv'd dark answers from *Appollo*'s shrine,
And honour'd him as Patron of their bliss;
So I, not muffled in simplicitie,
Zealous indeed of nothing but my good,
Hast to the *Augur* of my happiness,
To lay the ground of my ensuing Wars.
He learns his wisdom, not by flight of Birds,
By prying into sacrificed beasts,
By Hares that cross the way, by howling Wolves,
By gazing on the Starry Element,
Or vain imaginary calculations;
But from a setled wisdom in it self
Which teacheth to be void of passion.
To be Religious as the ravenous Wolf,
Who loves the Lamb for hunger, and for prey;
To threaten our inferiors with our looks;
To flatter our Superiors at our need;
To be an outward Saint, an inward Devill;
These are the lectures that my Master reads.
This Key commands all Chambers in the Court;
Now on a sudain will I try his wit,
I know my comming is unlook'd for.

   He opens the door, and finds Lorenzo *sleep a loft.*
Nay sleep, *Lorenzo*, I will walk a while.
As nature in the framing of the world,
Ordain'd there should be *nihil vacuum*;
Even so me thinks his wisdom shou'd contrive,
That all his Study should be full of wit,
And every corner stuft with sentences?
What's this? *Plato*? *Aristotle*? tush these are ordinary,
It seems this is a note but newly written. [*He reads a note
     which he finds among his Books.*

       Una

Emperour of Germany. 3

Una arbusta non alit duos Erithicos; *which being granted, the Roman Empire will not suffice* Alphonsus *King of* Castile, *and* Richard *Earl of* Cornwall *his competitor; thy wisdom teacheth thee to cleave to the strongest;* Alphonsus *is in possession, and therefore the strongest, but he is in hatred with the Electors, and men rather honour the Sun rising than the Sun going down.* I marry this is argued like himself, and now me thinks he wakes.

[*Lorenzo* Riseth; and snatches at his sword which hung by his Bed-side.]

Loren. What are there thieves within the Emperour's Court? Villain thou dy'st; what mak'st thou in my Chamber?

Alphon. How now *Lorenzo*, wilt thou slay thy Lord?

Loren. I do beseech your sacred Majesty to pardon me, I did not know your grace.

Alphon. Ly down *Lorenzo*, I will sit by thee,
The ayr is sharp and piercing; tremble not,
Had it been any other but our self,
He must have been a villain and a thief.

Loren. A.as my Lord! what means your excellence,
To walk by night in these so dangerous times?

Alphon. Have I not reason now to walk and watch,
When I am compast with so many foes?
They ward, they watch, they cast, and they conspire,
To win confederate Princes to their aid,
And batter down the Eagle from my creast.
O my *Lorenzo*, if thou help me not,
Th' Imperial Crown is shaken from my head,
And giv'n from me unto an English Earl.
Thou knowest how all things stand as well as we,
Who are our enemies, and who our friends,
Who must be threatned, and who dallyed with,
Who won by words, and who by force of arms;
For all the honour I have done to thee.
Now speak, and speak to purpose in the cause;
Nay rest thy body, labour with thy brain,
And of thy words my self will be the scribe.

Loren. Why then my Lord, take Paper, Pen and Ink,
Write first this maxim, it shall do you good,

1. A Prince must be of the nature of the Lion and the Fox; but not the one without the other. *Alphon.*

Alphon. The Fox is subtil, but he wanteth force.
The Lion strong, but scorneth policie;
I'l imitate *Lysander* in this point,
And where the Lion's hide is thin and scant,
I'l firmly patch it with the Foxes fell.
Let it suffice I can be both in one.

   Loren. 2. A Prince above all things must seem devout, but there is nothing so dangerous to his state, as to regard his promise or his oath.

   Alphon. Tush, fear not me, my promises are sound,
But he that trusts them shall be sure to fail.

   Loren. Nay my good Lord, but that I know your Majesty,
To be a ready quickwitted Scholar,
I would bestow a comment on the text.

   3. Trust not a reconciled friend; for good turns cannot blot out old grudges.

   Alphon. Then must I watch the Palatine of the *Rhein*,
I caus'd his Father to be put to death.

   Loren. Your Highness hath as little cause to trust
The dangerous mighty Duke of *Saxony*;
You know, you sought to banish him the Land;
And as for *Cullen*, was not he the first
That sent for *Richard* into *Germany*?

   Alphon. What's thy opinion of the other four?

   Alphon. That *Boheme* neither cares for one nor other,
But hopes this deadly strife between you twain,
Will cast th' Imperial Crown upon his head.
For *Trier* and *Brandenberg*, I think of them
As simple men that wish the common good;
And as for *Mentz* I need not censure him,
Richard hath chain'd him in a golden bond,
And sav'd his life from ignominious death.

   Alphon. Let it suffice, *Lorenzo*, that I know,
When *Churfurst Mentz* was taken Prisoner,
By young victorious *Otho* Duke of *Brunschweige*
That *Richard* Earl of *Cornwall* did disburse
The ransome of a King, a million,
To save his life, and rid him out of bands,
That sum of gold did fill the *Brunschweige* bags;
But since my self have rain'd a golden shower.

Of bright Hungarian Ducates and Crusadoes,
Into the private Coffers of the Bishop,
The English Angels took their wings and fled;
My crosses bless his Coffers and plead for me,
His Voice is mine, bought with ten tun of Gold,
And at the meeting of the seven Electors,
His Princely double-dealing holiness
Will spoyl the English Empereur of hope.
But I refer these matters to the sequel.
Proceed *Lorenzo* forward to the next.

 Loren. I'm glad your grace hath dealt so cunningly,
With that victorious fickle-minded Prelate; for in election
his voice is first but to the next.

 4. 'Tis more safety for a Prince to be feared than loved.

 Alphon. Love is an humour pleaseth him that loves;
Let me be hated, so I please my self.
Love is an humour mild and changeable;
But fear engraves a reverence in the heart.

 Loren. 5. To keep an usurped Crown, a Prince must
swear, forswear, poyson, murder, and commit all kind of villanies, provided it be cunningly kept from the eye of the world.

 Alphon. But my *Lorenzo* that's the hardest point,
It is not for a Prince to execute,
Physicians and Apothecaries must know,
And servile fear or Counsel-breaking bribes,
Will from a Peasant in an hour extort
Enough to overthrow a Monarchy.

 Loren. Therefore my Lord set down this Fixt and last Article.

 6. Be alwaies jealous of him that knows your secrets,
And therefore it behooves you credit few;
And when you grow into the least suspect,
With silent cunning must you cut them off.
As for example, *Julio Lentulus*,
A most renowned *Neapolitan*,
Gave me this Box of poyson, t'was not long
But therewithall I sent him to his grave.

 Alphon. And what's the special vertue of the same?
 Loren. That it is twenty dayes before it works.
 Alphon. But what is this?   *Loren.*

Loren. This an infection that kils suddainly;
This but a toy to cast a man asleep.
   Alphon. How? being drunk?
   Loren. No, being smelt unto.
   Alphon. Then smell *Lorenzo*, I did break thy sleep;
And for this time, this lecture shall suffice.
   Loran. What have you done my Lord? y'ave made me safe,
For stirring hence these four and twenty hours.
   Alphon. I see this charms his senses sudainly.
How now *Lorenzo*, half asleep already?
Æneas Pilot by the God of dreams,
Was never lull'd into a sounder trance;
And now *Alphonsus* over-read thy notes.   [*He reads.*
These are already at my fingers ends,
And lest the word should find this little Schedule,
Thus will I rend the text. and after this,
On my behaviour set so fair a glofs,
That men shall take me for a Convertite;
But some may think, I should forget my part,
And have been over rash in renting it,
To put them out of doubt I study sure,
I'le make a backward repetition,
In being jealous of my Counsel keepers,
This is the poyson that kils sudainly,
So didst thou unto *Julius Lentulus*,
And blood with blood must be requited thus.
Now am I safe, and no man knows my Counsels.
Churfurst of *Mentz*, if now thou play thy part,
Erning thy gold with cunning workmanship,
Upon the Bemish Kings ambition,
Richard shall shamefully fail of his hope,
And I with triumph keep my Emperie.   *Exit.*

Enter the King of Bohemia, *the Bishops of* Mentz, Collen,
  Trier, *the Pallatine of the* Rhein, *The Duke of* Saxon,
    The Marquess of Brandenburg.

   Bohe. *Churfursts* and Princes of the Election,
Since by the adverse fortune of our age,
The sacred and Imperial Majesty

                              Hath

Emperour of Germany.

Hath been usurp'd by open Tyranny,
We the seven Pillars of the German Empire,
To whom successively it doth belong
To make election of our Emperours,
Are here assembled to unite a new
Unto her former strength and glorious type,
Our half declining Roman Monarchy,
And in that hope, I *Henry* King of *Bohem,*
Churfurst and Sewer to the Emperour,
Do take my seat next to the sacred throne.

Mentz. Next seat belongs to *Julius Florius*
Archbishop of *Mentz*, Chancelor of *Germany*,
By birth the Duke of fruitful *Pomerland*.

Pal. The next place in election longs to me,
George Cassimirus Palsgrave of the *Rhein*,
His Highness Taster, and upon my knee
I vow a pure sincere innated zeal
Unto my Country, and no wrested hate,
Or private love shall blind mine intellect.

Collen. Brave Duke of *Saxon*, Dutchlands greatest hope,
Stir now or never, let the Spanish tyrant,
That hath dishonoured us, murder'd our Friends,
And stain'd this seat with blood of innocents,
At last be chastis'd with the *Saxon* sword,
And may *Albertus* Archbishop of *Collen*,
Chancelor of *Gallia* and the fourth Elector;
Be thought unworthy of his place and birth,
But he assist thee to his utmost power.

Sax. Wisdom, not words, must be the soveraign salve,
To search and heal these grievous festred wounds,
And in that hope *Augustus* Duke of *Saxon,*
Arch-Marshall to the Emperour take my place.

Trier. The like doth *Frederick* Arch-Bishop of *Trier*,
Duke of *Lorrain*, Chancelour of *Italie.*

Bran. The seventh and last is *Joachim Carolus,*
Marquess of *Brandenburg*, overworn with age,
Whose Office is to be the Treasurer;
But Wars have made the Coffers like the Chair.
Peace bringeth plenty, Wars bring poverty;
Grant Heavens, this meeting may be to effect,
Establish Peace, and cut off Tyrannie.   *Enter*

ALPHONSUS

Enter the Empreß Isabella *King* John's *Daughter*

Empreß. Pardon my bold intrusion mighty *Churfursts*,
And let my words pierce deeply in your hearts.
O! I beseech you on my bended Knees,
I the poor miserable Empress,
A stranger in this Land, unus'd to broyls,
Wife to the one, and Sister to the other
That are Competitors for Soveraignty;
All that I pray, is, make a quiet end;
Make Peace between my Husband and my Brother.
O think how grief doth stand on either side,
If either party chance to be amiss;
My Husband is my Husband; but my Brother,
My heart doth melt to think he should miscarry.
My Brother is my Brother; but my Husband,
O how my joynts do shake fearing his wrong!
If both should dye in these uncertain broyls.
O me, why do I live to think upon't!
Bear with my interrupted speeches Lords,
Tears stop my voice, your wisdoms know my meaning.
Alas I know my Brother *Richard*'s heart
Affects not Empire, he would rather choose
To make return again to *Palestine*,
And be a scourge unto the Infidels;
As for my Lord, he is impatient,
The more my grief, the lesser is my hope.
Yet Princes thus he sends you word by me,
He will submit himself to your award,
And labour to amend what is amiss.
All I have said, or can device to say,
Is few words of great worth, Make unity.

Bohe. Madam, that we have suffer'd you to kneel so long
Agrees not with your dignity nor ours;
Thus we excuse it, when we once are set,
In solemn Councel of Election,
We may not rise till somewhat be concluded.
So much for that; touching your earnest sute;
Your Majestie doth know how it concerns us,
Comfort your self, as we do hope the best;

But

Emperour of Germany.

But tell us, Madam, wher's your Husband now?
  Empreß. I left him at his prayers, good my Lord.
  Saxon. At prayers? Madam, that's a miracle.
  Pall. Vndoubtedly your Highnefs did miftake;
'Twas fure fome Book of Conjuration;
I think he never faid pray'r in his life.
  Empreß. Ah me, my fear, I fear, will take effect,
Your hate to him, and love unto my Brother,
Will break my heart, and fpoil th' Imperial peace.
  Mentz. My Lord of *Saxon*, and Prince *Pallatine*.
This hard opinion yet is more than needs;
But, gracious Madam, leave us to our felves.
  Empreß. I go, and Heav'n that holds the Hearts of Kings,
Direct your Counfels unto unity.   *Exit.*
  Bohe. Now to the depth of that we have in hand;
This is the queftion, whether the King of *Spain*
Shall ftill continue in the Royal throne,
Or yield it up unto *Plantagenet*,
Or we proceed unto a third Eelection.
  Saxon. E're fuch a viperous blood-thirfty **Spaniard**
Shall fuck the hearts of our Nobility,
Th' Imperial Sword which *Saxony* doth bear,
Shall be unfheath'd to War againft the world.
  Pall. My hate is more than words can teftifie,
Slave as he is he murdered my Father.
  Coll. Prince *Richard* is the Champion of the world,
Learned, and mild, fit for the Government.
  Bohe. And what have we to do with **Englifhmen**?
They are divided from our Continent.
But now that we may orderly proceed
To our high Office of Election,
To you my Lord of *Mentz* it doth belong,
Having firft voice in this Imperial Synod,
To name a worthy man for Emperour.
  Mentz. It may be thought, moft grave and reverend Prin- (ces,
That in refpect of divers fums of gold,
Which *Richard* of meer charitable love,
Not as a bribe, but as a deed of Alms,
Disburs'd for me unto the Duke of *Brunfchweige*,
That I dare name no other man but he,
                   C   Or

Or should I nominate an other Prince,
Upon the contrary I may be thought
A most ingrateful wretch unto my Friend ;
But private cause must yield to publick good ;
Therefore me thinks it were the fittest course,
To choose the worthiest upon this Bench.

   Bohem. We are all Germans, why should we be yoak'd
Either by Englishmen or Spaniards ?

   Saxo. The Earl of *Cornwall* by a full consent
Was sent for out of *England.*

   Mentz. Though he were,
Our later thoughts are purer than our first,
And to conclude, I think this end were best,
Since we have once chosen him Emperour,
That some great Prince of wisdom and of power,
Whose countenance may overbear his pride,
Be joynd in equal Government with *Alphonsus.*

   Bohem. Your Holiness hath soundly in few words
Set down a mean to quiet all these broyls.

   Trier. So may we hope for peace if he amend ;
But shall Prince *Richard* then be joynd with him ?

   Pal. Why should your Highness ask that question ?
As if a Prince of so high Kingly Birth,
Would live in couples with so base a Cur ?

   Bohe. Prince *Pallatine,* such words do ill become thee.

   Saxon. He said but right, and call'd a Dog a Dog.

   Bohe. His Birth is Princely.

   Saxo. His manners villanous,
And vertuous *Richard* scorns so base a yoak.

   Bohe. My Lord of *Saxon,* give me leave to tell you,
Ambition blinds your judgement in this case ;
You hope, if by your means *Richard* be Emperour,
He, in requital of so great advancement,
Will make the long-desired Marriage up
Between the Prince of *England* and your Sister,
And to that end *Edward* the Prince of *Wales,*
Hath born his Uncle Company to *Germany.*

   Saxo. Why King of *Bohem* i'st unknown to thee,
How oft the *Saxons* Sons have marryed Queens,
And Daughters Kings, yea mightiest Emperours ?

If

If *Edward* like her beauty and behaviour,
He'l make no question of her Princely Birth;
But let that pass, I say, as erst I said,
That vertuous *Richard* scorns so base a yoak.

   Mentz. If *Richard* scorn, some one upon this **Bench**,
Whose power may overbear *Alphonsus* pride,
Is to be named. What think you my Lords?

   Saxon. I think it was a mighty mass of Gold,
That made your grace of this opinion.

   Mentz. My Lord of *Saxony*, you wrong me much,
And know I highly scorn to take a bribe.

   Pal. I think you scorn indeed to have it known:
But to the purpose, if it must be so,
Who is the fittest man to joyn with him?

   Collen. First with an Oxe to plough will I be yok'd

   Mentz. The fittest is your grace in mine opinion.

   Bohem. I am content, to stay these mutinies,
To take upon me what you do impose.

   Saxon. Why here's a tempest quickly overblown,
God give you joy my Lord of half the Empire;
For me I will not meddle in the matter,
But warn your Majestie to have a care,
And vigilant respect unto your person,
I'l hie me home to fortifie my Towns,
Not to offend, but to defend my self.

   Palf. Ha' with you Cosin, and adieu my **Lords**,
I am afraid this suddain knitted Peace,
Will turn unto a tedious lasting War;
Only thus much we do request you all,
Deal honourably with the Earl of *Cornwall*,
And so adieu.   *Exeunt.* Saxon. *and* Palf.

   Brand. I like not this strange Farewel of the **Dukes**.

   Bohem. In all elections some are malcontent.
It doth concern us now with speed to know,
How the Competitors will like of this,
And therefore you my Lord Archbishop of *Trier*,
Impart this order of arbitrament
Unto the Emperour, bid him be content,
To stand content with half, or lose the whole.
My Lord of *Mentz* go you unto Prince *Richard*,

And tell him flatly here's no Crown, nor Empire
For English Islanders; tell him, 'twere his best,
To hie him home to help the King his Brother,
Against the Earl of *Leicester* and the Barons.
    Collen. My Lord of *Mentz*, sweet words will qualifie,
When bitter tearms will adde unto his rage.
'Tis no small hope that hath deceiv'd the Duke;
Therefore be mild; I know an Englishman,
Being flattered, is a Lamb, threatned, a Lion;
Tell him his charges what so e're they are
Shalbe repaid with treble vantages;
Do this; we will expect their resolutions.
    Mentz. Brother of *Collen*, I entreat your grace
To take this charge upon you in my stead;
For why I shame to look him in the face.
    Collen. Your Holiness shall pardon me in this,
Had I the profit I would take the pains;
With shame enough your Grace may bring the message.
    Mentz. Thus am I wrong'd, God knows, unguiltily.
    Brand. Then arm your countenance with innocency,
And boldly do the message to the Prince;
For no man else will be the messenger.
    Mentz. Why then I must, since ther's no remedy. [*Exit*
    Brand. If Heav'n that guides the hearts of   [*Mentz*
mighty men,
Do calm the Winds of these great Potentates,
And make them like of this Arbitrament,
Sweet Peace will tryumph thorough Christendom,
And *Germany* shall bless this happy day.

        Enter Alexander de Toledo *the Page.*

    Alexand. O me most miserable! O my dear Father!
    Bohem. What means this passionate accent? what art thou
That sounds these acclamations in our ears?
    Alex. Pardon me Princes, I have lost a Father,
O me, the name of Father kils my heart.
O! I shall never see my Father more,
H'as tane his leave of me for age and age.
    Collen. What was thy Father?
    Alex. Ah me! what was a not?

                                      Noble.

Emperour of Germany.

Noble, Rich, valiant, well-belov'd of all,
The glory and the wisdom of his age,
Chief Secretary to the Emperour.

Collen. Lorenzo *de Toledo*, is he dead?

Alex. Dead, ay me dead, ay me my life is dead,
Strangely this night bereft of breath and sense,
And I, poor I, am comforted in nothing,
But that the Emperour laments with me,
As I exclame, so he, he rings his hands,
And makes me mad to see his Majesty
Excruciate himself with endless sorrow.

Collen. The happiest news that ever I did hear
Thy Father was a villain murderer,
Witty, not wise, lov'd like a Scorpion,
Grown rich by the impoverishing of others,
The chiefest cause of all these mutinies,
And *Cæsar's* tutor to all villanie.

Alex. None but an open lyar terms him so.

Col. What Boy, so malepert?

Bohem. Good *Collen* bear with him, it was his Father,
Dutch-land is blessed in *Lorenzo's* Death.

Brand. Did never live a viler minded man.

Exeunt. Manet Alex.

Alex. Nor King, nor *Churfurst* should be privileg'd
To call me Boy, and rayl upon my Father,
Were I wehrsafflig; but in *Germany*,
A man must be a Boy at 40. years,
And dares not draw his weapon at a Dog,
Till being soundly box'd about the ears,
His Lord and Master gird him with a sword;
The time will come I shall be made a man,
Till then I'l pine with thought of dire revenge,
And live in Hell untill I take revenge.

ACT.

ACT. II.

Enter Alphonsus, Richard *Earl of* Cornwall, Mentz, Trier, *Prince* Edward, Bohemia, Collen, Brandenburge, *Attendants, and Pages with a sword.*

Bohem. Behold here come the Princes hand in hand,
Pleas'd highly with the sentence as it seems.
  Alphon. Princes and Pillars of the Monarchy,
We do admire your wisdoms in this cause,
And do accept the King of *Bohemia*,
As worthy partner in the Government.
Alas my Lords, I flatly now confess,
I was alone too weak to underprop
So great a burden as the Roman Empire,
And hope to make you all admire the course
That we intend in this conjunction.
  Richard. That I was call'd from *England* with consent
Of all the seven Electors to this place,
Your selves best know, who wrote for me to come.
'Twas no ambition mov'd me to the journey,
But pitty of your half declining State;
Which being likely now to be repayr'd,
By the united force of these two Kings,
I rest content to see you satisfied.
  Mentz. Brave Earl, wonder of Princely patience,
I hope your grace will not mis-think of me,
Who for your good, and for the Empires best,
Bethought this means to set the world at Peace.   (upon,
  Edward. No doubt this means might have been thought
Although your Holiness had dy'd in Prison.
  Mentz. Peace, peace young Prince, you want experience;
Your Unckle knows what cares accompany,
And wait upon the Crowns of mightiest Kings,
And glad he is that he hath shak'd it off.
  Edward. Heark in your ear my Lord, hear me one word,
Although it were more than a million,
Which these two Kings bestow'd upon your grace,
Mine Unckle *Richards* million sav'd your life.
  Mentz. You were best to say, your Unckle brib'd me then.   *Edward.*

Edward. I do but say mine Vnckle sav'd your life,
You know Count *Mansfield* your fellow Prisoner,
Was by the Duke of *Brunschwig* put to death.
   Mentz. You are a Child my Lord, your words are wind.
   Edward. You are a Fox my Lord, and past a Child.
   Bohem. My Lord of *Cornwall*, your great forwardness,
Crossing the Seas with aid of Englishmen,
Is more than we can any way requite;
But this your admirable patience,
In being pleas'd with our election,
Deserves far more than thanks can satisfie,
In any thing command the Emperours,
Who live to honour *Richard* Earl of *Cornwall*.
   Alpho. Our deeds shall make our Protestations good,
Mean while, brave Princes, let us leave this place,
And solace us with joy of this accord.

Enter Isabella *the Empress,* Hedewick *the Duke of* Saxon's
*Daughter, apparelled like Fortune, drawn on a Globe,
with a Cup in her hand, wherein are Bay leaves,
whereupon are written the lots. A train
of Ladies following with Musick.*

   Empress. To gratulate this unexpected Peace,
This glorious league confi'm'd against all hope,
Joyful *Isabella* doth present this shew,
Of Fortunes triumph, as the custom is
At Coronation of our Emperours;
If therefore every party be well pleas'd,
And stand content with this arbitriment,
Then daign to do as your Progenitors,
And draw in sequence Lots for Offices.
   Alphon. This is an order here in *Germany*,
For Princes to disport themselves with all,
In sign their hearts so firmly are conjoyn'd,
That they will bear a Fortunes equally,
And that the world may know I scorn no state,
Or course of life to do the Empire good,
I take my chance: My Fortune is to be the Forrester.
   Emp. If we want Venson either red or fallow,

                                                                  Wild

Wild bore or bear, you muſt be fin'd my Lord.
  Bohem. The Emperour's Taſter I.
  Emp. Your Majeſty hath been taſted to ſo oft,
That you have need of ſmall inſtructions.
  Richard. I am the bowr, Siſter what is my charge?
  Emp. Tyr'd like a Carter, and a Clowniſh Bowr,
To bring a load of Wood into the Kitchin.
Now for my ſelf, Faith I am Chamber Maid,
I know my charge; proceed unto the next.
  Alphon. Prince *Edward* ſtandeth melancholy ſtill,
Pleaſe it your Grace, my Lord, to draw your lot.
  Emp. Nephew you muſt be ſolemn with the ſad,
And given to myrth in ſportful Company,
The German Princes when they will be luſty,
Shake of all cares, and Clowns and they are Fellows.
  Edward. Sweet Aunt, I do not know the Country guiſe,
Yet would be glad to learn all faſhions.
Since I am next, good Fortune be my guide.
  Brand. A moſt ingenuous countenance hath this Prince,
Worthy to be the King of *England*'s Heir.
  Edward. Be it no diſparagement to you my Lords,
I am your Emperour.
  Alphon. Sound trumpets, God ſave the Emperour.
  Collen. The world could never worſe have fitted me,
I am not old enough to be the Cook.
  Empreß. If you be Cook, there is no remedy
But you muſt dreſs one Meſs of meat your ſelf.
  Branden. I am Phyſician.
  Trier. I am Secretary.
  Mentz. I am the Jeſter.
  Edward. O excellent! is your Holineſs the Vice?
Fortune hath fitted you y'faith my Lord,
You'l play the Ambodexter cunningly.
  Mentz. Your Highneſs is to bitter in your Jeſts.
  Alphon. Come hither *Alexander*, to comfort thee,
After the death of thy beloved Father,
Whoſe life was deer unto his Emperour,
Thou ſhalt make one in this ſolemnity,
Yet e're thou draw, my ſelf will honour thee,
And as the cuſtom is make thee a man.

Stand

Emperour of Germany.

Stand ſtiff Sir Boy, now com'ſt thou to thy tryal;
Take this, and that, and therewithall this Sword; [*He gives A-*
If while thou live, thou ever take the like, *lexander a*
Of me, or any man, I here pronounce *Box on the*
Thou art a ſchelm, otherwiſe a man. *ear or two.*
Now draw thy lot, and Fortune be thy ſpeed.

Edward. Vnckle I pray why did be box the fellow?
Foul lubber as he is, to take ſuch blows.

Richard. Thus do the Princes make their Pages men.

Edward. But that is ſtrange to make a man with blows.
We ſay in *England* that he is a man,
That like a man dare meet his enemy,
And in my judgement 'tis the ſounder tryal.

Alex. Fortune hath made me Marſhall of the tryumphs.

Alphon. Now what remains?

Empereß. That Fortune draw her lot.

She opens it, and gives it to the Empereß to read.

Empreß. Sound trumpets, Fortune is your Empereſs.

Alphon. This happens right; for Fortune will be Queen.
Now Emperour you muſt unmask her face,
And tell us how you like your Empereſs,
In my opinion *England* breeds no fairer.

Bohe. Fair *Hedewick* the Duke of *Saxons* daughter,
Young Prince of *England*, you are bravely match'd.

Edward. Tell me ſweet Aunt, is that this *Saxon* Princeſs,
Whoſe beauties fame made *Edward* croſs the Seas?

Empereß. Nephew, it is; hath fame been prodigal,
Or over ſparing in the Princeſs praiſe?

Edward. Fame I accuſe thee, thou did'ſt niggardize,
And faintly ſound my loves perfections.
Great Lady Fortune, and fair Empereſs,
Whom chance this day hath thrown into my arms,
More welcome than the Roman Empereſs. [*Edward k ſ-*

Hed.. Şee dooh. daſs iſt hier kein gebzanch, *ſes her.*
Mein Got iſt daſs dir Engliſch manier, daſs dich.

Edward. What meaneth this? why chafes my Empereſs?

Alphon. Now by my troth, I did expect this jeſt,
Prince *Edward* us'd his Country faſhion.

Edward. I am an Engliſhman, why ſhould I not?

D

Emp. Fy Nephew *Edward,* here in *Germany*
To kiss a Maid, a fault intollerable.
  Edward. Why should not *German* Maids be kist aswell as others?
  Richard. Nephew, because you did not know the fashion,
And want the language to excuse your self,
I'l be your spokes-man to your Emperess.
  Edward. Excuse it thus: I like the first so well,
That tell her, she shall chide me twice as much
For such an other; nay tell her more than so,
I'l double kiss on kiss, and give her leave
To chide and braul, and cry ten thousand Dats dich,
And make her weary of her fretting humour,
E're I be weary of my kissing vein,
Dats dich a Jungfraw angry for a kiss.
  Empreß. Nephew, she thinks you mock her in her mirth.
  Edward. I think the Princes make a scorn of me.
If any do, I'l prove it with my Sword,
That English Courtship leaves it from the world.
  Bohem. The pleasant'st accident that I have seen.
  Bran. Me thinks the Prince is chaf'd as well as she.
  Rich. Gnediges frawlin.
  Hede. Dats dich, mast ich arme kindt zu schanden gemacht werden.
  Edward. Dats dich I have kist as good as you,
Pray Unckle tell her; if she mislike the kiss,
I'l take it off agen with such an other.
  Rich. Ey Liebes frawlin nhm es all für gutt
Es ist die Englisch munier Und gebzauche.
  Hede. Ewer gnaden weißts woll es ist mir ein grosse schande.   (pardon.
  Edward. Good Aunt teach me so much Dutch to ask her
  Empreß. Say so: Gnediges frawlin vergebet mirs, ich wills nimmermehz thuen,
Then kiss your hand three times upfy Dutch.   (right,
  Edward. Ich wills nimmermehz thuen, if I understand it,
That's as much to say, as I'l do so no more.
  Empr. True Nephew.
  Edward. Nay Aunt pardon me I pray, I hope to kiss her many thousand times,

And

Emperour of Germany.   19

And shall I go to her like a great Boy, and say I'l do so no more.

 Empreß. I pray Cosin say as I tell you.

 Edward. Gnediges frawlin vergebet mirs ich wills nimmermehr thuen.

 Alphou. For wahr kein schandt.

 Hedew. Gnediger hochgeborner Fürst vndt herr wan ich konte so vil englisch sprechen ich wolt ewer Gnaden.

Fur wahr ein flitz geben, ich hoffe aber ich soll einmahl So viel lernen dass Die mich verstehen soll.

 Edward. What says she?

 Alphon. O excellent young Prince look to your self,
She swears she'l learn some English for your sake,
To make you understand her when she chides.

 Edward. I'l teach her English, she shall teach me Dutch,
Gnediges frawlin, &c.

 Bohem. It is great pitty that the Duke of *Saxon,*
Is absent at this joyful accident,
I see no reason if his Grace were here,
But that the Marriage might be solemniz'd,
I think the Prince of *Wales* were well content.

 Edward. I left sweet *England* to none other end;
And though the Prince her Father be not here,
This Royal presence knows his mind in this.

 Emp. Since you do come so roundly to the purpose,
'Tis time for me to speak, the Maid is mine,
Giv'n freely by her Father unto me,
And to the end these broyls may have an end,
I give the Father's interest and mine own,
Unto my Nephew *Edward* Prince of *Wales.*

 Edward. A Jewel of incomparable price,
Your Majesty hath here bestowed on me,
How shall I ask her if she be content?

 Empr. Say thus, ist ewer gnaden woll hiemit zufrieden.

 Edward. Ist ewer Gnaden woll hiemit zufrieden.

 Hede. Wass ihr durleichtigkeit dass will dass will mein vatter vndt
Wass mein vatter will darmit muss ich zufrieden sein.

 Alphon. It is enough, she doth confirm the match;

D 2   We

ALPHONSUS

We will dispatch a Post unto her Father,
On Sunday shall the Revels and the Wedding,
Be both solemnized with mutual joy.
Sound trumpets, each one look unto his charge,
For preparation of the Festivals. *Exeunt.*

Manent Alphonsus *and* Alexander.

Alphon. Come hither *Alexander*, thy Fathers joy:
If tears and sighs, and deep-fetcht deadly groans,
Could serve t' evert inexorable fate,
Divine *Lorenzo*, whom in life my heart,
In death my soul and better part adores,
Had to thy comfort and his Prince's honour,
Surviv'd, and drawn this day this breath of life.

Alexan. Dread *Cæsar*, prostrate on my bended Knee,
I thank your Majesty for all favours shewn
To my deceased Father and my self.
I must confess, I spend but bootless tears,
Yet cannot bridle nature, I must weep,
Or heart will break with burden of my thoughts,
Nor am I yet so young or fond withall,
Causless to spend my gall, and fret my heart,
'Tis not that he is dead, for all must dye;
But that I live to hear his lives reproach.
O sacred Emperour, these ears have heard,
What no Sons ears can unrevenged hear,
The Princes all of them, but specially,
The Prince Elector Archbishop of *Collen*,
Revil'd him by the names of murderer,
Arch villain, robber of the Empires fame,
And *Cæsars* tutor in all wickedness,
And with a general voice applaus'd his death,
As for a special good to Christendome.

Alphon. Have they not reason to applaud the deed
Which they themselves have plotted? ah my Boy,
Thou art too young to dive into their drifts.

Alex. Yet old enough I hope to be reveng'd.

Alphon. What wilt thou do, or whither wilt thou run?

Alex. Headlong to bring them death, then dye my self.

Alphon. First hear the reason why I do mistrust them.

Alex

Alex. They had no reason for my Father's death,
And I scorn reason till they all be dead.
 Alphon. Thou wilt not scorn my Counsel in revenge?
 Alex. My rage admits no Counsel but revenge.
 Alphon. First let me tell thee whom I do mistrust.
 Alex. Your Highness said you did mistrust t'em all.
 Alpho. Yea *Alexander*, all of them, and more than all,
My most especiall neerest dearest friends.
 Alex. All 's one to me, for know thou Emperour,
Were it thy Father, Brother, or thine Empress,
Yea were 't thy self, that did'st conspire his death,
This fatal hand should take away thy life.
 Alphon. Spoke like a Son, worthy so dear a Father,
Be still and hearken, I will tell thee all,
The Duke of *Saxon*---
 Alex. O, I thought no less.
 Alphon. Suppress thy choler, hearken to the rest.
Saxon I say so wrought with flattering *Mentz*,
Mentz with *Bohemia*, *Trier*, and *Brandenburg*,
For *Collen* and the *Palsgrave* of the *Rhein*
Were principals with *Saxon* in the Plot,
That in a general meeting to that purpose,
The seven selected Emperours electors,
Most hainously concluded of the murder;
The reason why they doom'd him unto death,
Was his deep wisdom and sound policy;
Knowing while he did live my state was firm,
He being dead my hope must dye with him.
Now *Alexander* will we be reveng'd
Upon this wicked whore of *Babylon*,
This hideous monster with the seven-fold head;
We must with cunning level at the heart,
With pierc'd and perisht all the body dyes:
Or strike we off her heads by one and one,
Behooveth us to use dexterity,
Lest she do trample us under her feet,
And tryumph in our honours overthrow.
 Alex. Mad and amaz'd to hear this tragick doom,
I do subscribe unto your sound advice.   (tence,
 Alphon. Then hear the rest; these seven gave but the sen-

A neerer hand put it in execution,
And but I lov'd *Lorenzo* as my life,
I never would betray my dearest Wife.

   Alex. What? what the Empress accessary to?

   Alphon. What cannot kindred do? her Brother *Richard*,
Hoping thereby to be an Emperour,
Gave her a dram that sent him to his grave.

   Alex. O my poor Father, wert thou such an eye-sore,
That 9. the greatest Princes of the earth
Must be confederate in thy tragedy?
But why do I respect their mightiness,
Who did not once respect my Fathers life?
Your Majesty may take it as you please,
I'l be reveng'd upon your Emperess,
On English *Richard*, *Saxon*, and the Palsgrave,
On *Bohem*, *Collen*, *Mentz*, *Trier*, and *Brandenburg*,
If that the Pope of *Rome* himself were one
In this confederacy, undaunted I,
Amidst the College of his Cardinals,
Would press, and stab him in St. *Peters* chair,
Though clad in all his *Pontificalibus*.

   Alphon. Why *Alexander*? do'st thou speak to me
As if thou didst mistrust my forwardness?
No, thou shalt know my love to him was such,
And in my heart I have proscrib'd them all,
That had to do in this conspiracy.
The bands of Wedlock shall not serve her turn,
Her fatal lot is cast among the rest,
And to conclude, my soul doth live in Hell
Till I have set my foot upon their necks,
That gave this spur of sorrow to my heart;
But with advice it must be managed,
Not with a head-long rage as thou intend'st,
Nor in a moment can it be perform'd,
This work requires long time, dissembling looks,
Commixt with undermining actions,
Watching advantages to execute.
Our foes are mighty, and their number great,
It therefore follows that our Stratagems
Must branch forth into manifold deceits,

                                 Endless

Emperour of Germany.   23

Endless devices, bottomless conclusions.
   Alexan. What by your Majesty is prescrib'd to me,
That will I execute or dye the death.
I am content to suck my sorrows up,
And with dull patience will attend the time,
Gaping for every opportunity
That may present the least occasion;
Although each minute multiply mine anguish,
And to my view present a thousand forms
Of senseless bodies in my Fathers shape,
Yelling with open throat for just revenge.
   Alphon. Content thy self, he shall not cry in vain,
I have already plotted *Richards* death.
   Alex. That hath my Fathers sacred Ghost inspir'd,
O tell me, shall I stab him suddainly?
The time seems long, till I be set a work.
   Alphon. Thou knowest in griping at our lots to day,
It was Prince *Richard's* hap to be the bowr;
So that his Office is to drive the Cart,
And bring a load of Wood into the Kitchin.
   Alex. O excellent, your Grace being Forester,
As in the thicket he doth load the Cart,
May shoot him dead, as if he were a Deer.
   Alphon. No *Alexander*, that device were shallow,
Thus it must be, there are two very bowrs
Appointed for to help him in the Wood,
These must be brib'd or cunningly seduc'd,
Instead of helping him to murder him.
   Ale. Verbum satis sapiens, it is enough,
Fortune hath made me Marshal of the sports
I hope to Marshal them to th' Devils Feast.
Plot you the rest, this will I execute,
Dutch bowrs as towsandt schelms and gold to tempt them.
   Alphon. 'Tis right, about it then, but cunningly.
   Alex. Else let me lose that good opinion
Which by your Highness I desire to hold,
By Letters which I'l strew within the Wood,
I'l undermine the bowrs to murder him,
Nor shall they know who set them so a work,
Like a familiar will I fly about,

                                         And

And nimbly haunt their Ghosts in every nook.
Exit. Manet Alphonsus.

Alphon. This one nayl helps to drive the other out,
I slew the Father, and bewitch the Son,
With power of words to be the instrument
To rid my foes with danger of his life.
How easily can subtil age intice,
Such credulous young novices to their death?
Huge wonders will *Alphonsus* bring to pass,
By the mad mind of this enraged Boy;
Even they which think themselves my greatest friends,
Shall fall by this deceit, yea my Arch-enemies
Shall turn to be my chief confederates.
My sollitary walks may breed suspect,
I'le therefore give my self to Companie,
As I intended nothing but these sports,
Yet hope to send most actors in this Pageant,
To Revel it with *Rhadamant* in Hell. *Exit.*

Enter Richard *Earl of* Cornwall *like a Clown*.

Richard. How far is *Richard* now unlike the man
That crost the Seas to win an Emperie?
But as I plod it like a plumper Bowr,
To fetch in Fewel for the Kitchin fire,
So every one in his vocation,
Labours to make the pastimes plausible;
My Nephew *Edward* jets it through the Court,
With Princess *Hedewick* Empress of his Fortune
The demy *Cæsar* in his hunters suit,
Makes all the Court to Ring with Horns and Hounds,
Collen the Cook bestirs him in the Kitchin;
But that which joyes me most in all these sports,
Is *Mentz*, to see how he is made an Ass?
The common scorn and by-word of the Court;
And every one to be the same he seems,
Seems to forget to be the same he is.
Yet to my roabs I cannot suit my mind,
Nor with my habit shake dishonour off.
The seven Electors promis'd me the Empire,
The perjur'd Bishop *Mentz* did swear no less

Yet

Emperour of Germany.

Yet I have seen it shar'd before my face,
While my best friends do hide their heads for shame;
I bear a shew of outward full content,
But grief thereof hath almost kill'd my heart.
Here rest thee *Richard*, think upon a mean,
To end thy life, or to repair thine honour,
And vow never to see fair *Englands* bounds,
Till thou in *Aix* be Crowned Emperour.

Enter two Bowrs.

Holla, me thinks there cometh Company,
The Bowrs I troe that come to hew the Wood,
Which I must carry to the Kitchen Fire,
I'le lye a while and listen to their talk.

Enter Hans and Jerick two Dutch Bowrs.

Je. Kom hier hans wo?e bist dow, warumb bist sow so traw?ick? biss frolick kan wel gelt verdienen, wir wil ihr bey potts tawsandt todt schlagen.

Han. Lat mich die brieffe sehen.

Rich. Me thinks they talk of murdering some body, I'l listen more.

Reads the Letter.

Hans vnd Jerick, mein liebe fremde, ich bitte lasset es bey euch bleiben in geheim, vnd schlaget den Engellander zu todt.

Rich. What's that? *Hans* vnd *Jerick* my good friend, I pray be secret and murder the Englishman.

Jerick reads.

Hear weiter, den er ist kein bow?e nicht, er ist ein Juncker, vnd hatt viel gelt vnd kleinothen bey sich.

Rich. For he is no Bowre but a Gentleman, and hath store of Gold and Jewels by him.

Jeric Noch weiter: ihr solt solche gelegenheit nicht versahmen, vnd wan ihr gethan habet, ich will euch sagen, was ich fur ein guter Karl bin, der euch raht gegeben habe.

Rich. Slip not this opportunity, and when you have done, I will discover who gave you the Counsel.

Jerick. Wat sagst dow, wilt dow es thun?

Hans. Wat will ich nich fur gelt thun? see potts tausendt, dar ist er.

E Jerick?

Jerick. Ja, bey potts taufends flapperment, er ists, holla guter morgen, gluck zu Juncker.

Hans. Juncker, der divell he is ein bowre!

Rich. Dow bist ein schelm, weich von mir.

Jerick. Holla, holla, bist dow so hoffertick? Juncker bowre, kompt hier, oder diese vnd jenner felleuch holen.

Rich. Ich bien ein Furst, brieb mich nicht ihr schelms, ihr verrahters.

Bath. Sla to, sla to, wir will yow furstlick tracteren.

Richard having nothing in his hand but his whip, defends himself a while, and then fall's down, as if he were dead:

Rich. O Got, nimb meine seele in deine hande.

Jerick. O excellent, hurtick he is todt, he is todt. Lat vns see, wat he hat for gelt bey sich, holla hier is all enough, all satt, dor is for dich, and dor is for mich, vnd dit will ich darto haben:

Jerick puts the chain about his neck.

Hans. How so Hans Harhals, geue mir die kette hier.

Jerick. Ja ein dreck, dit kett stehet hupsch vmb mein hals, dit will ich tragen.

Hans. Dat dich potts velten leiden dat soltu nimmermehr thun dow schelm.

Jerick. Wat solt dow mich schelm hetten, nimb dat.

Hans. Dat dich hundert tonnen divells, harr ich will dich lernen.

Jerick. Wilstud hawen oder stechen?

Hans. Ich will redlich hawen;

Jerick. Nun wollan, dar ist mein ruck, sla to.

They must have axes made for the nonst to fight withall, and while one strikes, the other holds his back without defence.

Hans: Nimb dow das, vnd dar hast mein ruck.

Jerick. Noch amahl: O excellent, ligst dow dar, nun will ich alles haben gelt vnd kett, vnd alle mit einander, O hurtig frisch vp lustig, nun bin ich ein hurtig Juncker.

Richard rises up again and snatcheth up the fellows hatchet that was slain.

Rich. *Nè Hercules contra duos*, yet polliey hath gone beyond them both.

Du

Emperour of Germany.   27

Du buler schelm, morder, kehre dich, seestu mich? gebe
mir die kett und gelt wieder;

  Jerick. Wat bistu wieder lebendig worden, so mus ich
meren, wat wiltu stechen oder hawen?

  Richard. So will ich machen du schelm

  Jerick. Harr, harr, bistu ein redlich karle, so ficht redlich,
O ich sterb, ich sterb, lat mich leben

  Richard. Sagt mir dan wer hatt die brieffe geschrieben?
Lie nicht sondern sagt die warheit:

  Jerick. O mein fromer, guter, edler, gestrenger Juncker,
dar ist dat gelt und kett wieder, yow soll alles haben, aber
wer hatt die brieffe geschrieben, dat wet ich bey meiner seele
nicht.

  Rich. Lig dor still, still ich sag.
The villain swears, and deeply doth protest
He knows not who incited them to this,
And as it seems the scrowl imports no less.
So sterb du mir schelm.

  Jerick. O ich sterb, awe, awe, awe dat dich der divell
hole!

As Richard *kils the* Bowr. *Enter* Saxon *and the* Palsgrave.

  Saxon. Fy dich an loser schelm, hastu dein gesellen todt
geschlagen?

  Palsgr. Last us den schelmen angreiffen.

  Richard. Call you me shelme how dare you then
Being Princes offer to lay hands on me?
That is the Hangmans Office here in Dutch-land.

  Saxon. But this is strange, our Bours can speak no Eng-
lish,
What bistum more than a damn'd murderer?
That thou art so much we are witnesses.

  Rich. Can then this habit alter me so much,
That I am call'd a villain by my friends?
Or shall I dare once to suspect your graces,
That for you could not make me Emperour,
Pittying my sorrow through mine honour lost,
You set these slaves to rid me of my life,
Yet far be such a thought from *Richard*'s heart.

                    E 2   *Pals.*

Pals. How now? what do I hear Prince *Richard* speak?
Rich. The same: but wonder that he lives to speak.
And had not policy helpt above strength,
These sturdy swains had rid me of my life.
  Sax. Far be it from your Grace for to suspect us.
  Rich. Alas, I know not whom I should suspect;
But yet my heart cannot misdoubt your Graces?
  Saxon. How came your Highness into this apparrel?
  Rich. We as the manner is drew lots for Offices,
My hap was hardest to be made a Carter,
And by this letter which some villain wrote,
I was betray'd, here to be murdered;
But Heav'n which doth defend the Innocent,
Arm'd me with strength and policy together,
That I escap'd out of their treacherous snare.
  Pals. Were it well founded, I dare lay my life,
The *Spanish* tyrant knew of this conspiracie;
Therefore the better to dive into the depth
Of this most devillish murderous complot,
As also secretly to be beholders,
Of the long-wisht for wedding of your daughter
We will disrobe these bowrs of their apparrel,
Clapping their rustick cases on our backs,
And help your Highness for to drive the Cart.
T'may be the traytor that did write these lines,
Mistaking us for them will shew himself.
  Richard. Prince *Palatine* this plot doth please me well,
I make no doubt if we deal cunningly,
But we shall find the writer of this scroul.
  Saxon. And in that hope I will disrobe this slave.
Come Princes in the neighbouring thicket here,
We may disguise our selves, and talk at pleasure;
Fye on him heavy lubber how he weighs.
  Richard. The sin of murder hangs upon his soul,
It is no mervail then if he be heavy.   *Exeunt.*

A C

ACT. III.

Enter to the Revels.

Edward *with an Imperial Crown.* Hedewig *the Empress* Bohemia *the Taster.* Alphonsus *the Forrester.* Mentz *the Gester.* Empress *the Chambermaid.* Brandenburg *Physician.* Tryer *Secretarie.* Alexander *the Marshal, with his Marshals staff, and all the rest in their proper apparrel, and Attendants and Pages.*

Alex. Princes and Princes Superiors, Lords and Lords fellows, Gentlemen and Gentlemens Masters, and all the rest of the States here assembled, as well Masculine as Feminine, be it known unto you by these presence, that I *Alexander de Toledo*, Fortunes chief Marshal do will and command you, by the authority of my said Office, to take your places in manner and form following, First the Emperour and the Empress, then the Taster, the Secretary the Forrester, the Physician, as for the Chambermaid and my self, we will take our places at the neither end, the Jester is to wait up, and live by the crums that fall from the Emperours trencher, But now I have Marshal'd you to the table, what remains?

Mentz. Every fool can tell that, when men are set to dinner they commonly expect an eat.

Edward. That's the best Jest the fool made since he came into his Office. Marshal walk into the Kitchin, and see how the *Churfurst* of *Collen* bestirs himself.   *Exit.* Alex.

Mentz. Shall I go with him too? I love to be imploy'd in the Kitchin.

Edward. I prethee go, that we may be rid of thy wicked Jests.

Mentz. Have with thee Marshal, the fool rides thee.
   Exit. on Alex. *back.*

Alphon.

Alphon. Now by mine honour, my Lord of *Mentz* plays the fool the worst that ever I saw.

Edward. He do's all by contraries; for I am sure he playd the wiseman like a fool, and now he plays the fool wisely.

Alphon. Princes and *Churfursts* let us frolick now,
This is a joyful day to Christendome,
When Christian Princes joyn in amity,
Schinck bowls of Reinsal and the purest Wine,
We'l spend this evening lustie upsie Dutch,
In honour of this unexpected league.

Empres. Nay gentle Forrester, there you range amiss,
His looks are fitly suited to his thoughts,
His glorious Empress makes his heart tryumph,
And hearts tryumphing makes his countenance stai'd,
In contemplation of his lives delight.

Edward. Good Aunt let me excuse my self in this,
I am an Emperour but for a day,
She Empress of my heart while life doth last;
Then give me leave to use Imperial looks,
Nay if I be an Emperour I'l take leave,
And here I do pronounce it openly,
What I have lately whisper'd in her ears,
I love mine Empress more than Empery,
I love her looks above my fortunes hope.   (bowl,

Alphon. Saving your looks dread Emperour es gelt a
Unto the health of your fair Bride and Empress.

Edward. Sain Got es foll mir en liebe dzunk sein, so much Dutch have I learnt since I came into *Germany*.

Bran. When you have drunk a dozen of these bowls,
So can your Majesty with a full mouth,
Trowl out high Dutch, till then it sounds not right.
Dzauff es gelt noch eins ihr Majestat.

Edward. Sain Got lass lauffen.

Bohem. My Lord of *Brandenburg* spoken like a good Dutch Brother;
But most unlike a good Physician,
You should consider what he has to do,
His Bride will give you little thanks to night.

Alphon. Ha, ha my Lord, now give me leave to laugh,
He need not therefore shun one Beaker full.

In

Emperour of Germany.

In *Saxon* Land you know it is the use,
That the first night the Bridegroom spares the Bride.
  Bohem. 'Tis true indeed, that had I quite forgotten.
  Edward. How understand I that?
  Alphon. That the first night,
The Bride and Bridegroom never sleep together.
  Edward. That may well be, perchance they wake together.
  Bohem. Nay without fallace they have several Beds.
  Edward. I in one Chamber, that is most Princely.
  Alphan. Not onely several Beds, but several Chambers,
Lockt soundly too, with Iron Bolts and Bars.
  Empr. Beleeve me Nephew, that's the custom here.
  Edward. O my good Aunt, the world is now grown new,
Old customs are but superstitions.
I 'm sure this day, this presence all can witness,
The high and mighty Prince th' Archbishop of *Collen,*
Who now is busie in the skullery,
Joyn'd us together in St. *Peters* Church,
And he that would disjoyn us two to night,
'Twixt jest and earnest be it proudly spoken,
Shall eat a piece of ill-digesting Iron.
Bride wilt dow dis nicht ben mee schlapen.
  Hede. Da behute mich Gott fur, Ich hoffe Eure majestat
wills von mir nist, begeran.
  Edward. What says the behute mich Got fur?
  Alphon. She says God bless her from such a deed.
  Edward. Tush Empress, clap thy hands upon thy head,
And God will bless thee, I have a *Jacobs* staff,
Shall take the Elevation of the Pole;
For I have heard it sayd, the Dutch North star,
Is a degree or two higher than ours.
  Bohem. Nay though we talk lets drink, and Emperour,
I'l tell you p'ainly what you must trust unto,
Can they deceive you of your Bride to night,
They'll surely do't, therefore look to your self.
  Edward. If she deceive me not, let all do their worst.
  Alphon. Assure you Emperour she'l do her best.
  Edward. I think the Maids in *Germany* are mad,
E're they be marryed they will not kiss,
And being marryed will not go to Bed.

                                                    We

We drink about, let's talk no more of this,
Well warn'd half arm'd our English proverb say
    Alphon. Holla Marshal, what says the Cook?
            Enter Alexander.
Belike he thinks we have fed so well already,
That we disdain his simple Cookery.
    Alex. Faith the Cook says so, that his Office was to dress a mess of meat with that Wood which the English Prince should bring in, but he hath neither seen Dutch Wood nor English Prince, therefore he desires you hold him excus'd.
    Alphon. I wonder where Prince *Richard* stays so long.
    Alex. An't, please your Majesty, he's come at length,
And with him has he brought a crew of Bowrs,
A hipse bowr maikins fresh as Flow'rs in *May*,
With whom they mean to dance a *Saxon* round,
In honour of the Bridegroom and his Bride.
    Edward. So has he made amends for his long tarrying.
I prethee Marshall them into the presence.
    Alphon. Lives *Richard* then? I had thought th' had'st made him sure.
    Alex. O I could tear my flesh to think upon 't,
He lives and secretly hath brought with him,
The *Palsgrave* and the Duke of *Saxonie*,
Clad like two Bowrs, even in the same apparrel   (him,
That *Hans* and *Jerick* wore when they went out to murder
It now behooves us to be circumspect.
    Alphon. It likes me not; Away Marshal bring them.
                  Exit. Alexander.
I long to see this sports conclusion.
    Bohem. I'st not a lovely sight to see this couple
Sit sweetly billing like two Turtle Doves.
    Alphon. I promise you it sets my Teeth an Edge,
That I must take mine Empress in mine arms.
Come hither *Isabel*, though thy roabs be homely,
Thy face and countenance holds colour still.

                                Enter

Emperour of Germany.   33

Enter Alexander, Collen, Mentz, Richard, Saxony, Palſgrave, Collen Cook, *with a gamon of raw bacon, and
links or puddings in a platter,* Richard, Palſgrave,
Saxon, Mentz, *like Clowns with each of them
a Miter with Coranees
on their heads.*

  Collen. Dread Emperour and Empereſs fot to day,
I Your appointed Cook untill to morrow,
Have by the Marſhal ſent my juſt excuſe,
And hope your Highneſs is therewith content,
Our Carter here for whom I now do ſpeak,
Says that his Axletree broke by the way,
That is his anſwer, and for you ſhall not famiſh,
He and his fellow bowrs of the next dorp,
Have brought a ſchinkel of good raw Bacon,
And that's a common meat with us, unſod,
Deſiring you, you would not ſcorn the fare,
'Twil make a cup of Wine taſte nippitate.
  Edward. Welcome good fellows, we thank you for your preſent.
  Richard. So ſpell freſh up and let us rommer daunſen.
  Alex. Pleaſe it your Highneſs to dance with your Bride?
  Edward. Alas I cannot dance your *German* dances.
  Bohem. I do beſeech your Highneſs mock us not,
We *Germans* have no changes in our dances,
An Almain and an upſpring that is all,
So dance the Princes, Burgers, and the Bowrs.
  Brand. So daunc'd our Aunceſtors for thouſand years
  Edward. It is a ſign the Dutch are not newfangled.
I'le follow in the meaſure; Marſhal lead.

Alexander *and* Mentz *have the fore dance with each of them
a glaſs of Wine in their hands, then* Edward *and* Hedewick,
Palſgrave *and* Empreſs, *and two other couple, after
Drum and Trumpet.*

  The Palſgrave *whiſpers with the* Empreſs.
  Alphon. I think the Bowr is amorous of my Empreſs.
Fort bows and leffel morgen, when thou com'ſt to houſe.
  Collen. Now is your Graces time to ſteal away,
           F   Look

ALPHONSUS

Look to't or else you'l lie alone to night.

Edvard steals away the Bride.

Alex. (Drinketh to the Palsgrave.) 𝕾𝖐𝖊𝖑𝖙 𝖇𝖔𝖜𝖗𝖊.

Palsgrave. 𝕳𝖆𝖎𝖓 𝕲𝖔𝖙𝖙.

The Palsgrave requests the Empress.

𝕰𝖞 𝕵𝖚𝖓𝖌𝖋𝖗𝖆𝖜 𝖍𝖊𝖑𝖕𝖊 𝖒𝖎𝖈𝖍 𝖉𝖔𝖈𝖍 𝖊𝖎𝖓 𝕵𝖚𝖓𝖌𝖋𝖗𝖆𝖜 𝖉𝖗𝖚𝖓𝖈𝖐
𝕰𝖘 𝖌𝖊𝖑𝖙 𝖌𝖚𝖙𝖊𝖗 𝖋𝖈𝖊𝖓𝖚𝖉𝖙 𝖊𝖎𝖓 𝖋𝖗𝖔𝖑𝖔𝖈𝖐𝖊𝖓 𝖉𝖗𝖎𝖓𝖐. (thun

Alphon. 𝕳𝖆𝖒 𝕲𝖔𝖙𝖙 𝖒𝖊𝖎𝖓 𝖋𝖗𝖚𝖓𝖉𝖙 𝖎𝖈𝖍 𝖜𝖎𝖑𝖑 𝖌𝖊𝖗𝖓 𝖇𝖊𝖋𝖈𝖍𝖊𝖗𝖔𝖙

(*Alphonsus takes the Cup of the Palsgrave, and drinks to the King of Bohemia, and after he hath drunk puts poyson into the Beaker.*)

Half this I drink unto your Highness health,
It is the first since we were joynd in Office.

Bohem. I thank your Majesty, I'le pledge you half.

(*As Bohem is a drinking, e're he hath drunk it all out, Alphonsus pulls the Beaker from his mouth.*)

Alphon. Hold, hold, your Majesty, drink not too much.

Bohem. What means your Highness. (teeth,

Alphon. Methinks that something grates between my
Pray God there be not poyson in the bowl.

Bohem. Marry God forbid.

Alex. So were I pepper'd.

Alphon. I highly do mistrust this fchelmish bowr,
Lay hands on him, I'le make him drink the rest.

𝖂𝖍𝖆𝖘 𝖎𝖋𝖋 𝖜𝖍𝖆𝖘 𝖎𝖋𝖋 𝖜𝖆𝖙 𝖜𝖎𝖑𝖑 𝖞𝖔𝖚 𝖓𝖚𝖙 𝖒𝖊𝖊 𝖒𝖆𝖈𝖍𝖊𝖓

Alphon. Drink out, drink out 𝖔𝖉𝖊𝖗 𝖉𝖊𝖗 𝖉𝖎𝖛𝖊𝖑𝖑 𝖋𝖔𝖑𝖑 𝖉𝖎𝖈𝖍 𝖍𝖔𝖑𝖊𝖓.

Palf. 𝕰𝖞 𝖌𝖊𝖇 𝖞𝖔𝖚 𝖙𝖔 𝖋𝖗𝖎𝖊𝖉𝖊𝖓 𝖎𝖈𝖍 𝖜𝖎𝖑𝖑 𝖌𝖊𝖎𝖓 𝖉𝖗𝖎𝖓𝖐. (ground,

Saxon. Drink not Prince *Pallatine*, throw it on the
It is not good to trust his Spanish flies.

Bohem. Saxon and *Palsgrave*, this cannot be good.

Alphon. 'Twas not for nought my mind misgave me so;
This hath Prince *Richard* done t'entrap our lives.

Richard. No *Alphonsus*, I disdain to be a traytor.

Empress. O sheath your swords, forbear these needless broyls.

Alphon. Away, I do mistrust thee as the rest.

Bohem. Lord's hear me speak, to pacify these broyls;
For my part I feel no distemperature,
How do you feel your self?

Alphon. I cannot tell, not ill, and yet methinks I am not well. *Bohem.*

Emperour of Germany.   35

Bohem. Were it a poyson 'twould begin to work.
Alphon. Not so, all poysons do not work alike.
Palf. If there were poyson in, which God forbid,
The Empress and my self and *Alexander*,
Have cause to fear as well as any other.
Alphon. Why didst thou throw the Wine upon the earth?
Hadst thou but drunk, thou hadst satisfied our minds.
Palf. I will not be enforc't by Spanish hands.
Alphon. If all be well with us, that schuce shall serve,
If not, the Spaniards blood will be reveng'd.
Rich. Your Majesty is more afraid than hurt.
Bohem. For me I do not fear my self a whit,
Let all be friends, and forward with our mirth.

Enter Edward *in his night-gown and his shirt.*

Richard. Nephew, how now? is all well with you?
Bohem. I lay my life the Prince has lost his bride.
Edward. I hope not so, she is but stray'd a little.
Alphon. Your Grace must not be angry though we laugh.
Edward. If it had hapned by default of mine,
You might have worthily laught me to scorn;
But to be so deceiv'd, so over reach'd,
Even as I meant to clasp her in mine arms,
The grief is intollerable, not to be guest,
Or comprehended by the thought of any,
But by a man that hath been so deceiv'd,
And that's by no man living but my self.
Saxon. My Princely Son-in-Law God give you joy.
Edward. Of what my Princely Father?
Saxon. O' my Daughter.
Your new betroathed Wife and Bed-fellow.
Edward. I thank you Father, indeed I must confess
She is my Wife, but not my Bed-fellow.
Saxon. How so young Prince? I saw you steal her hence,
And as me thought she went full willingly.
Edward. 'Tis true, I stole her finely from amongst you,
And by the Arch Bishop of *Collens* help,
Got her alone into the Bride-Chamber,
Where having lockt the Door, thought all was well.
I could not speak but pointed to the Bed,

F 2   She

She answered *Ia* and gan for to unlace her;
I seeing that suspected no deceit,
But straight untrust my points, uncas'd my self,
And in a moment slipt between the Sheets;
There lying in deep contemplation,
The Princess of her self drew neer to me,
Gave me her hand, spake prettily in Dutch
I know not what, and kist me lovingly,
And as I shrank out of my luke warm place
To make her room, she clapt thrice with her feet,
And through a trap-door sunck out of my sight;
Knew I but her Confederates in the deed---
I say no more.
   Empress. Tush Cosin, be content;
So many Lands, so many fashions,
It is the *German* use, be not impatient,
She will be so much welcomer to morrow.
   Rich. Come Nephew, we'l be Bed-fellows to night.
   Edward. Nay if I find her not, I'le lye alone,
I have good hope to ferret out her Bed,
And so good night sweet Princess all at once.
   Alphon. Godnight to all; Marshal discharge the train.
   Aex. To Bed, to Bed the Marshal crys 'tis time. *Exeunt*

   Flourish Cornets, Manent Saxon, Richard, Palsgrave,
            Collen, Empress.

   Saxon. Now Princes it is time that we advise,
Now we are all fast in the Fowlers gin,
Not to escape his subtle snares alive,
Unless by force we break the Nets asunder.
When he begins to cavil and pick quarrels,
I will not trust him in the least degree.
   Empress. It may beseem me evill to mistrust
My Lord and Emperour of so foul a fact;
But love unto his honour and your lives,
Makes me with tears intreat your Excellencies
To fly with speed out of his dangerous reach,
His cloudy brow foretells a suddain storm
Of blood not natural but prodigious.
   Rich. The Castle gates are shut, how should we fly

But

Emperour of Germany.   37

But were they open, I would lose my life,
E're I would leave my Nephew to the slaughter;
He and his Bride were sure to bear the brunt.
  Saxon. Could I get out of doors, I'ld venture that,
And yet I hold their persons dear enough,
I would not doubt, but e're the morning Sun
Should half way run his course into the South.
To compass and begirt him in his Fort,
With *Saxon* lansknights and brunt-bearing *Switzers*,
Who lye in Ambuscado not far hence,
That he should come to Composition.
And with safe conduct bring into our tents,
Both Bride and Bridegroom, and all other friends.
  Empress. My Chamber Window stands upon the Wall,
And thence with ease you may escape away.
  Saxon. Prince *Richard*, you will bear me Company?
  Richard. I will my Lord.
  Saxon. And you Prince *Pallatine?*
  Palf. The Spanish Tyrant hath me in suspect
Of poysoning him, I'l therefore stay it out,
To fly upon't were to accuse my self.
  Empress. If need require, I'le hide the *Pallatine,*
Untill to morrow, if you stay no longer.
  Saxon. If God be with us, e're to morrow noon,
We'll be with Ensigns spread before the Walls,
We leave dear pledges of our quick return.
  Emp. May the Heavens prosper your just intents. *Exeunt.*

Enter Alphonsus.

  Alphon. This dangerous plot was happily overheard,
Here didst thou listen in a blessed howr.
Alexander, where do'st thou hide thy self?
I've sought thee in each Corner of the Court,
And now or never must thou play the man.
  Alex. And now or never must your Highness stir,
Treason hath round encompassed your life.
  Alphon. I have no leasure now to hear thy talk.
Seest thou this Key?
  Alex. Intends your Majesty that I should steal into the Princes Chambers,

F 3   And

And sleeping stab them in their Beds to night?
That cannot be.
   Alphon. Wilt thou not hear me speak?
   Alex. The Prince of *England, Saxon,* and of *Collen,*
Are in the Empress Chamber privily.
   Alphon. All this is nothing, they would murder me,
I come not there to night; seest thou this Key?
   Alex. They mean to fly out at the Chamber Window,
And raise an Army to beseech your Grace,
Now may your Highness take them with the deed.
   Alphon. The Prince of *Wales* I hope is none of them.
   Alex. Him and his Bride by force they will recover.
   Alphon. What makes the cursed *Palsgrave* of the *Rhein* ?
   Alex. Him hath the Empress taken to her charge,
And in her Closet means to hide him safe.
   Alphon. To hide him in her Closet ? of bold deeds,
The dearest charge that e're she undertook,
Well let them bring their Complots to an end,
I'le undermine to meet them in their works,
   Alex. Will not your Grace surprize them e're they fly ?
   Alphon. No, let them bring their purpose to effect,
I'le fall upon them at my best advantage,
Seest thou this Key ? there take it *Alexander;*
Yet take it not unless thou be resolv'd :
Tush I am fond to make a doubt of thee ;
Take it I say, it doth command all Doors,
And will make open way to dire revenge.
   Alex. I know not what your Majesty doth mean.
   Alphon. Hie thee with speed into the inner Chamber,
Next to the Chappel, and there shalt thou find
The danty trembling Bride coutcht in her Bed,
Having beguil'd her Bridegroom of his hopes,
Taking her farewel of Virginity,
Which she to morrow night expects to lose,
By night all Cats are gray, and in the dark,
She will imbrace thee for the Prince of *Wales,*
Thinking that he hath found her Chamber out,
Fall to thy business and make few words.
And having pleas'd thy senses with delight,

                                      And

And fild thy beating vains with stealing joy,
Make thence agen before the break of day,
What strange events will follow this device,
We need not study on, our foes shall find.
How now? how standst thou? hast thou not the heart?
　Alex. Should I not have the heart to do this deed,
I were a Bastard villain and no man;
Her sweetness, and the sweetness of revenge,
Tickles my senses in a double sense,
And so I wish your Majesty good night.
　Alphon. God night, sweet *Venus* prosper thy attempt.
　Alex. Sweet *Venus* and grim *Ate* I implore,
Stand both of you to me auspicious.　　*Exit.* Alexander.
　Alphon. It had been pitty of his Fathers life,
Whose death hath made him such a perfect villain.
What murder, wrack, and causeless enmity,
'Twixt dearest friends that are my strongest foes,
Will follow suddainly upon this rape;
I hope to live to see, and laugh thereat,
And yet this peece of practice is not all.
The King of *Bohem* though he little feel it,
Because in twenty hours it will not work,
Hath from my Knives point suck'd his deadly bane,
Whereof I will be least of all suspected;
For I will feign my self as sick as he,
And blind mine enemies eyes with deadly groans;
Upon the *Palsgrave* and mine Emperess,
Heavy suspect shall light to bruze their bones;
Though *Saxon* would not suffer him to taste,
The deadly potion provided for him
He cannot save him from the Sword of Iustice,
When all the world shall think that like a villain,
He hath poyson'd two great Emperours with one draught;
That deed is done, and by this time I hope,
The other is a doing, *Alexander*
I doubt it not will do it thorowly.
While these things are a brewing I'l not sleep,
But sudainly break ope the Chamber doors,
And rush upon my Empress and the *Palsgrave*,

　　　　　　　　　　　　　　　　　Holla

ALPHONSUS

Holla wher's the Captain of the Guard?

Enter Captain, and Souldiers.

Cap. What would your Majesty?
Alphon. Take six travants well arm'd and followe,
They break with violence into the Chamber, and Alphonsus *trayls the Empress by the hair.*

Enter Alphonsus, *Empreß, Souldiers*, &c.

Alphon. Come forth thou damned Witch, adulterous Whore,
Foul scandal to thy name, thy sex, thy blood.
Emp. O Emperour, gentle Husband, pitty me.
Alphon. Canst thou deny thou wert confederate,
With my arch enemies that sought my blood?
And like a Strumpet through thy Chamber Window,
Hast with thine own hands helpt to let them down,
With an intent that they should gather arms,
Besiege my Court, and take away my life?
Emp. Ah my *Alphonsus*.
Alphon. Thy *Alphonsus* Whore?
Emp. O pierce my heart, trail me not by my hair;
What I have done, I did it for the best.
Alphon. So for the best advantage of thy lust,
Hast thou in secret *Clytemnestra* like,
Hid thy *Ægestus* thy adulterous love.
Emp. Heav'n be the record 'twixt my Lord and me;
How pure and sacred I do hold thy Bed.
Alphon. Art thou so impudent to bely the deed,
Is not the *Palsgrave* hidden in thy Chamber?
Empe. That I have hid the *Palsgrave* I confess;
But to no ill intent your conscience knows.
Alphon. Thy treasons, murders, incests, sorceries,
Are all committed to a good intent;
Thou know'st he was my deadly enemy.
Emp. By this device I hop'd to make your friends.
Alphon. Then bring him forth, we'l reconcile our selves.
Emp. Should I betray so great a Prince's life?
Alphon. Thou holdst his life far dearer than thy Lords,
This very night hast thou betrayd my blood,

But

Emperour of Germany.

But thus, and thus, will I revenge my self,
And but thou speedily deliver him,
I'le trail thee through the Kennels of the Street,
And cut the Nose from thy bewitching face,
And into *England* send thee like a Strumpet
　Emp. Pull every hair from off my head,
Drag me at Horses tayls, cut off my nose
My Princely tongue shall not betray a Prince
　Alphon. That will I try.
　Emp. O Heav'n revenge my shame.

Enter Palsgrave.

　Pal. Is *Cæsar* now become a torturer,
A Hangman of his Wife, turn'd murderer?
Here is the *Pallatine*, what wouldst thou more?
　Alphon. Upon him Souldiers, strike him to the ground.
　Emp. Ah Souldiers, spare the Princely *Pallatine*.
　Alphon. Down with the damn'd adulterous murderer,
Kill him I say, his blood be on my head.

They kill the Pallatine.

Run to the Tow'r, and Ring the Larum Bell,
That fore the world I may excuse my self,
And tell the reason of this bloody deed.

Enter Edward *in his night gown and shirt.*

　Edw. How now? what means this sudain strange Allarm?
What wretched dame is this with blubbered cheeks,
And rent dishevel'd hair?
　Emp. O my dear Nephew,
Fly, fly the Shambles, for thy turn is next.
　Edward. What, my Imperial Aunt? then break my heart.
　Alphon. Brave Prince be still, as I am nobly born,
There is no ill intended to thy person.

Enter Mentz, Tryer, Branden. Bohem.

　Mentz. Where is my Page? bring me my two hand Sword.
　Tryer. What is the matter? is the Court a fire

G　　　　　　　　　　　　　*Bohem.*

ALPHONSUS

Bran. Whose that? the Emperour with his weapon drawn?
Bohem. Though deadly sick yet am I forc'd to rise,
To know the reason of this hurley burley.
  Alphon. Princes be silent, I will tell the cause,
Though sudainly a griping at my heart
Forbids my tongue his wonted course of speech.
See you this Harlot, traytress to my life,
See you this murderer stain to mine honour,
These twain I found together in my Bed,
Shamefully committing lewd Adultery,
And hainously conspiring all your deaths,
I mean your deaths, that are not dead already;
As for the King of *Boheme* and my self,
We are not of this world, we have our transports
Giv'n in the bowl by this adulterous Prince,
And least the poyson work too strong with me,
Before that I have warnd you of your harms,
I will be brief in the relation.
That he hath staind my Bed, these eyes have seen,
That he hath murder'd two Imperial Kings,
Our speedy deaths will be too sudain proof;
That he and she have bought and sold your lives,
To *Saxon*, *Collen*, and the English Prince,
Their Ensigns spread before the Walls to morrow
Will all too sudainly bid you defiance.
Now tell me Princes have I not just cause,
To slay the murderer of so many souls?
And have not all cause to applaud the deed?
More would I utter, but the poysons force
Forbids my speech, you can conceive the rest.
  Bohem. Your Majesty reach me your dying hand,
With thousand thanks for this so just revenge.
O, how the poysons force begins to work!
  Mentz. The world may pitty and applaud the deed.
  Brand. Did never age bring forth such hainous acts.
  Edward. My senses are confounded and amaz'd.
  Emp. The God of Heav'n knows my unguiltiness.
      Enter Messenger.
  Mes. Arm, arm my Lords, we have descry'd afar,

An

Emperour of Germany.

An Army of ten thousand men at arms.
   Alphon. Some run unto the Walls, some draw up the Sluce, Some speedily let the Purcullefs down.
   Mentz. Now may we see the Emperours words are true. To prison with the wicked murderous Whore.   *Exeunt.*

ACT. IV.

Enter Saxon *and* Richard *with Souldiers.*

   Saxon. My Lord of *Cornwall,* let us march before,
To speedy rescue of our dearest friends,
The rereward with the armed Legions,
Committed to the Prince of *Collen*'s charge,
Cannot so lightly pass the mountain tops.
   Richard. Let's summon sudainly unto a Parly,
I do not doubt but e're we need their helps,
Collen with all his forces will be here.

   Enter Collen *with Drums and an Army.*

   Richard. Your Holiness hath made good haft to day,
And like a beaten Souldier lead your troops.
   Collen. In time of peace I am an Arch-Bishop,
And like a Church-man can both sing and say;
But when the innocent do suffer wrong,
I cast my rocket off upon the Altar,
And like a Prince betake my self to arms.

   Enter above Mentz, Tryer, *and* Brandenburg.

   Mentz. Great Prince of *Saxonie,* what mean these arms?
Richard of *Cornwall,* what may this intend?
Brother of *Collen* no more Churchman now,
Instead of Miter, and a Croisier Staff,
Have you betane you to your Helm and Targe?
Were you so merry yesterday as friends,
Cloaking your treason in your Clowns attire?
   Saxon. Mentz, we return the traytor in thy face.
To save our lives, and to release our friends,

ALPHONSUS

Out of the Spaniards deadly trapping Snares,
Without intent of ill, this power is rais'd;
Therefore grave Prince Marquess of *Brandenburg*,
My loving Cosen, as indifferent Judge,
To you an aged Peace-maker we speak,
Deliver with safe conduct in our tents,
Prince *Edward* and his Bride, the *Pallatine*,
With every one of high or low degree,
That are suspicious of the King of *Spain*,
So shall you see that in the self same howr
We marched to the Walls with colours spread,
We will cashier our troups, and part good friends.

Brand. Alas my Lord, crave you the *Pallatine*?
Rich. If craving will not serve, we will command.
Brand. Ah me, since your departure, good my Lords,
Strange accidents of bloud and death are hapned.
Saxon. My mind misgave a massacre this night.
Rich. How do's Prince *Edward* then?
Sax. How do's my Daughter?
Collen. How goes it with the *Palsgrave* of the *Rhein*?
Brand. Prince *Edward* and his Bridle do live in health,
And shall be brought unto you when you please.
Saxon. Let them be presently deliver'd?
Coll. Lives not the *Palsgrave* too?
Mentz. In Heaven or Hell he lives, and reaps the merit of his deeds.
Coll. What damned hand hath butchered the Prince?
Saxon. O that demand is needless, who but he,
That seeks to be the Butcher of us all;
But vengeance and revenge shall light on him.
Bran. Be patient noble Princes, hear the rest.
The two great Kings of *Bohem* and *Castile*,
God comfort them, lie now at point of death,
Both poyson'd by the *Palsgrave* yesterday.
Rich. How is that possible? so must my Sister,
The *Pallatine* himself, and *Alexander*,
Who drunk out of the bowl, be poysoned too.
Mentz. Nor is that hainous deed alone the cause,
Though cause enough to ruin Monarchies;
He hath defil'd with lust th' Imperial Bed,

And

Emperour of Germany.

And by the Emperour in the fact was slain.
  Collen. O worthy guiltless Prince, O had he fled.
  Rich. But say where is the Empress, where's my Sister.
  Mentz. Not burnt to ashes yet, but shall be shortly.
  Rich. I hope her Majesty will live to see
A hundred thousand flattering turncoat slaves,
Such as your Holiness, dye a shameful death.
  Brand. She is in prison, and attends her tryal.
  Saxon. O strange heart-breaking mischievous intents,
Give me my children if you love your lives,
No safety is in this enchanted Fort.
O see in happy hour there comes my Daughter,
And loving son, scapt from the Massacre.

      Enter Edward *and* Hedewick.

  Edward. My body lives, although my heart be slain,
O Princes this hath been the dismali'st night,
That ever eye of sorrow did behold,
Here lay the *Palsgrave* weltring in his bloud,
Dying *Alphonsus* standing over him,
Upon the other hand the King of *Bohem,*
Still looking when his poyson'd bulk would break;
But that which pierc'd my soul with natures touch
Was my tormented Aunt with blubberd cheeks,
Torn bloody Garments, and dithevel'd hair,
Waiting for death; deservedly or no,
That knows the searcher of all humane thoughts;
For these devices are beyond my reach.   (mass.
  Saxon. Saſt doꝛh liebes dofſter who wart dow dicſelbir-
  Hede. Is who who ſolt ich ſem ich war in bette.
  Saxon. Wert dow allrin ſo wart dow gar vo ſchꝛocken.
  Hede. Ich ha miſt audes gemeint dam das ich wolt allein
geſſſlaffne haven, abur vmb mitternaiſt kam mriner bꝛidegroom
bundt ſiſlaffet bey mir, bis wir mit dem getunnuel
erwacht waren.   (midnight?
  Edward. What says she? came her Bridegroom to her at
  Rich. Nephew, I see you were not over-reach'd;
A though she slipt out of your arms at first,
You ceiz'd her surely, e're you left the chace.
  Saxon. But left your Grace your Bride alone in Bed?

Or did she run together in the Larum?
   Edward. Alas my Lords, this is no time to jest;
I lay full sadly in my Bed alone,
Not able for my life to sleep a wink,
Till that the Larum Bell began to Ring,
nd then I started from my weary couch.   (speech,
   Saxon. How now? this rimes not with my daughters
She says you found her Bed, and lay with her.
   Edward. Not I, your Highness did mistake her words.
   Collen. Deny it not Prince *Edward,* 'tis an honour.
   Edward. My Lords I know no reason to deny it;
T' have found her Bed, I wou'd have given a million. (*An.*
   Saxon. 𝔥𝔢𝔡𝔢𝔴𝔦𝔠𝔨 𝔡𝔢𝔯 𝔉𝔲𝔯𝔰𝔱 𝔰𝔞𝔤𝔱 𝔢𝔯 𝔰𝔞𝔱𝔱 𝔪𝔦𝔱𝔱 𝔟𝔢 𝔡𝔦𝔯 𝔰𝔠𝔥𝔩𝔞-
   Hede. 𝔈𝔰 𝔤𝔢𝔰𝔢𝔩𝔱 𝔦𝔥𝔪 𝔞𝔩𝔰𝔬 𝔷𝔲𝔪 𝔰𝔞𝔤𝔲𝔫 𝔞𝔟𝔢𝔯 𝔦𝔠𝔥 𝔥𝔞𝔟𝔢𝔰 𝔴𝔬𝔩𝔩
𝔤𝔢𝔯𝔣𝔯𝔞𝔩𝔢𝔱.
   Rich. She say's you are dispos'd to jest with her;
But yesternight she felt it in good earnest.
   Edward. Unckle these jests are too unsavorie,
Ill suited to these times, and please me not,
𝔏𝔞𝔟 𝔦𝔠𝔥 𝔟𝔦𝔫 you 𝔤𝔢𝔰𝔠𝔥𝔩𝔞𝔭𝔢𝔫 yesternight.
   Hede. 𝔍 𝔩𝔢𝔰𝔰, 𝔴𝔞𝔯𝔲𝔪 𝔰𝔫𝔦𝔱 𝔦𝔥𝔷𝔰 𝔣𝔯𝔞𝔤𝔢𝔫.
   Saxon. Edward, I tell thee 'tis no jesting matter,
Say plainly, wa'st thou by her I or no?
   Edward. As I am Prince, true heir to *Englands* Crown,
I never toucht her body in a Bed.
   Hede. 𝔇𝔞𝔰 𝔥𝔞𝔰𝔱𝔢 𝔤𝔢𝔱𝔥𝔞𝔫 𝔬𝔡𝔢𝔯 𝔥𝔬𝔩𝔩𝔢 𝔪𝔦𝔠𝔥 𝔡𝔢𝔯 𝔡𝔦𝔳𝔢𝔩𝔩.
   Richard. Nephew, take heed, you hear the Princess words.
   Edward. It is not she, nor you nor all the world,
Shall make me say I did anothers deed.
   Saxon. Anothers deed? what think'st thou her a whore?
                 Saxon strikes Edward.
   Edward. She may be Whore, and thou a villain too.
Strook me the Emperour I will strike again.
   Collen. Content you Princes, buffet not like boys.
   Richard. Hold you the one, and I will hold the other.
   Hede. 𝔒 𝔥𝔢𝔯 𝔤𝔬𝔱, 𝔥𝔢𝔩𝔭, 𝔥𝔢𝔩𝔭, 𝔬𝔦𝔠𝔥 𝔞𝔯𝔪𝔰 𝔨𝔦𝔫𝔡𝔱.
   Saxon. Souldiers lay hands upon the Prince of *Wales,*
Convey him speedily unto a prison,
And load his Legs with grievous bolts of Iron;
Some bring the Whore my Daughter from my sight;
And thou smooth Englishman to thee I speak,   My

Emperour of Germany. 47

My hate extends to all thy Nation,
Pack thee out of my sight, and that with speed
Your English practises have all to long,
Muffled our *German* eyes, pack, pack I say.
    Richard. Although your Grace have reason for your rage,
Yet be not like a madman to your friends.
    Saxon. My friends? I scorn the friendship of such mates,
That seek my Daughters spoil, and my dishonour;
But I will teach the Boy another lesson,
His head shall pay the ransom of his fault.
    Richard. His head?
    Saxon. And thy head too, O how my heart doth swell?
Was there no other Prince to mock but me?
First woo, then marry her, then lye with her,
And having had the pleasure of her Bed,
Call her a Whore in open audience,
None but a villain and a slave would do it,
My Lords of *Mentz,* of *Tryer,* and *Brandenburg,*
Make ope the Gates, receive me as a friend,
I'le be a scourge unto the English Nation.
    Mentz. Your Grace shall be the welcom'st guest alive,
    Collen. None but a madman would do such a deed.
    Saxon. Then *Collen* count me mad, for I will do it.
I'le set my life and Land upon the hazard,
But I will thoroughly sound this deceit.
What will your Grace leave me or follow me?
    Collen. No *Saxon,* know I will not follow thee,
And leave Prince *Richard* in so great extreams.
    Saxon. Then I defy you both, and so farwell.
    Rich. Yet *Saxon* hear me speak before thou go,
Look to the Princes life as to thine own,
Each perisht hair that falleth from his head
By thy default, shall cost a *Saxon* City,
Henry of *England* will not lose his heir,
And so farwel and think upon my words.
    Saxon. Away, I do disdain to answer thee.
Pack thee with shame again into thy Countrie,
I'le have a Cock-boat at my proper charge,
And send th' Imperial Crown which thou hast won,
To *England* by Prince *Edward* after thee.   *Exeunt.*
            Man. Rich. and *Coll.*   *Collen,*

Collen. Answer him not Prince *Richard*, he is mad,
Choler and grief have rob'd him of his senses.
Like accident to this was never heard.

   Rich. Break heart and dye, flie hence my troubled spirit,
I am not able for to underbear
The weight of sorrow which doth bruze my soul,
O *Edward*, O sweet *Edward*, O my life.
O noble *Collen* last of all my hopes,
The only friend in my extremities,
If thou doest love me, as I know thou doest,
Unsheath thy sword, and rid me of this sorrow.

   Collen. Away with abject thoughts, fie Princely *Richard*,
Rouze up thy self, and call thy senses home,
Shake of this base pusillanimitie,
And cast about to remedie these wrongs.

   Richard. Alas I see no means of remedie.

   Collen. Then hearken to my Counsel and advice,
We will Intrench our selves not far from hence,
With those small pow'rs we have, and send for more,
If they do make assault, we will defend;
If violence be offer'd to the Prince,
We'l rescue him with venture of our lives;
Let us with patience attend advantage,
Time may reveal the author of these treasons,
For why undoubtedly the sweet young Princess,
Fowly beguild by night with cunning shew,
Hath to some villain lost her Maiden-head.

   Rich. O that I knew the foul incestuous wretch,
Thus would I tear him with my teeth and nails.
Had *Saxon* sense he would conceave so much,
And not revenge on guiltless *Edwards* life.

   Collen. Perswade your self he will be twice advis'd,
Before he offer wrong unto the Prince.

   Rich. In that good hope I will have patience.
Come gentle Prince whose pitty to a stranger
Is rare and admirable, not to be spoken.
England cannot requite this gentleness.

   Collen. Tush talk not of requital, let us go,
To fortifie our selves within our trench.   *Exeunt.*

Enter

Enter Alphonso (*carried in the Couch*) Saxony, Mentz, Tryer, Brandenburg, Alexander.

 Alphon. O most excessive pain, O raging Fire!
Is burning *Cancer* or the *Scorpion*,
Descended from the Heavenly Zodiack,
To parch mine Entrals with a quenchless flame?
Drink, drink I say, give drink or I shall dye.
Fill a thousand bowls of Wine, Water I say
Water from forth the cold *Tartarian* hils.
I feel th' ascending flame lick up my blood,
Mine Entrals shrink together like a scrowl
Of burning parchment, and my Marrow fries,
Bring hugie Cakes of Ice, and Flakes of Snow,
That I may drink of them being dissolved.
 Saxon. We do beseech your Majestie have patience.
 Alphon. Had I but drunk an ordinary poyson,
The sight of thee great Duke of *Saxony*,
My friend in death, in life my greatest foe,
Might both allay the venom and the torment;
But that adulterous *Palsgrave* and my Wife,
Upon whose life and soul I vengeance cry,
Gave me a mineral not to be digested,
Which burning eats, and eating burns my heart.
My Lord of *Tryer*, run to the King of *Bohem*,
Commend me to him, ask him how he fares,
None but my self can rightly pitty him;
For none but we have sympathie of pains.
Tell him when he is dead, my time's not long,
And when I dye bid him prepare to follow. *Exit.* Tryer.
Now, now it works a fresh; are you my friends?
Then throw me on the cold swift running *Rhyn*,
And let me bath there for an hour or two,
I cannot bear this pain.
 Mentz. O would th' unpartial fates afflict on me,
These deadly pains, and ease my Emperour,
How willing would I bear them for his sake.
 Alphon. O *Mentz*, I would not wish unto a Dog,
The least of thousand torments that afflict me,
Much less unto your Princely holiness
      H   See

ALPHONSUS

See, see my Lord of *Mentz*, he points at you.

Mentz. It is your fantasie and nothing else;
But were death here, I would dispute with him,
And tell him to his teeth he doth unjustice,
To take your Majesty in the prime of youth;
Such wither'd rotten branches as my self,
Should first be lopt, had he not partial hands;
And here I do protest upon my Knee,
I would as willingly now leave my life,
To save my King and Emperour alive,
As erst my Mother brought me to the world.

Brand. My Lord of *Mentz*, this flattery is too gross,
A Prince of your experience and calling,
Should not so fondly call the Heavens to witness.

Mentz. Think you my Lord, I would not hold my word?

Brand. You know my Lord, death is a bitter guest.

Mentz. To ease his pain and save my Emperour,
I sweetly would embrace that bitterness.

Alex. If I were death, I knew what I would do.

Mentz. But see, his Majesty is faln a sleep,
Ah me. I fear it is a dying slumber.

Alphon. My Lord of *Saxonie* do you hear this jest.

Saxon. What should I hear my Lord?

Alphon. Do you not hear
How loudly death proclames it in mine ears,
Swearing by trophies, Tombs and deadmens Graves,
If I have any friend so dear to me,
That to excuse my life will lose his own,
I shall be presently restor'd to health.

Enter Tryer.

Mentz. I would he durst make good his promises.

Alphon. My Lord of *Tryer*, how fares my fellow Emperour?

Tryer. His Majesty is eas'd of all his pains.

Alphon. O happy news, now have I hope of health.

Mentz. My joyful heart doth spring within my bodie,
To hear those words,
Comfort your Majestie I will excuse you,
Or at the least will bear you Company.

Alphon.

Alphon. My hope is vain, now, now my heart will break,
My Lord of *Tryer* you did but flatter me,
Tell me the truth, how fares his Majestie.

Tryer. I told your Highnes, eas'd of all his pain.

Alphon. I understand thee now, he's eas'd by death,
And now I feel an alteration;
Farewel sweet Lords, farewel my Lord of *Mentz*,
The truest friend that ever earth did bear,
Live long in happines to revenge my death,
Upon my Wife and all the English brood.
My Lord of *Saxonie* your Grace hath cause.

Mentz. I dare thee death to take away my life.
Some charitable hand that loves his Prince,
And hath the heart, draw forth his Sword and rid me of my life.

Alex. I love my Prince, and have the heart to do it.

Mentz. O stay a while.

Alex. Nay now it is to late.

Bran. Villain what hast thou done? th'ast slain a Prince.

Alex. I did no more than he intreated me,

Alphon. How now, what make I in my Couch so late?
Princes why stand you so gazing about me?
Or who is that lies slain before my face?
O I have wrong, my soul was half in Heaven,
His holines did know the joys above,
And therefore is ascended in my stead.
Come Princes let us bear the body hence;
I'le spend a Million to embalm the same.
Let all the Bels within the Empire Ring,
Let Mass be said in every Church and Chappel,
And that I may perform my latest vow,
I will procure so much by Gold or friends,
That my sweet *Mentz* shall be Canonized,
And numbred in the Bed-role of the Saints;
I hope the Pope will not deny it me,
I'le build a Church in honour of thy name,
Within the antient famous Citie *Mentz*,
Fairer than any one in *Germany*,
There shalt thou be interrd with Kingly Pomp,
Over thy Tomb shall hang a sacred Lamp,

H 2   Which

Which till the day of doom shall ever burn,
Yea after ages shall speak of thy renown,
And go a Pilgrimage to thy sacred Tomb.
Grief stops my voice, who loves his Emperour,
Lay to his helping hand and bear him hence,
Sweet Father and redeemer of my life. *Exeunt.*

Manet *Alexander.*

Alex. Now is my Lord sole Emperour of *Rome*,
And three Conspirators of my Fathers death,
Are cunningly sent unto Heaven or Hell;
Like subtilty to this was never seen.
Alas poor *Mentz*! I pittying thy prayers,
Could do no less than lend a helping hand,
Thou wert a famous flatterer in thy life,
And now hast reapt the fruits thereof in death
But thou shalt be rewarded like a Saint,
With Masses, Bels, dirges and burning Lamps;
'Tis good, I envie not thy happiness :
But ah the sweet remembrance of that night,
That night I mean of sweetness and of stealth,
When for a Prince, a Princess did imbrace me,
Paying the first fruits of her Marriage Bed,
Makes me forget all other accidents.
O *Saxon* I would willingly forgive,
The deadly trespass of my Fathers death,
So I might have thy Daughter to my Wife,
And to be plain, I have best right unto her,
And love her best, and have deserv'd her best;
But thou art fond to think on such a match;
Thou must imagin nothing but revenge,
And if my computation fail me not,
Ere long I shall be thorowly reveng'd. *Exit.*

Enter *the Duke of* Saxon, *and* Hedewick *with the Child.*

Saxon. Come forth thou perfect map of miserie,
Desolate Daughter and distressed Mother,
In whom the Father and the Son are curst;
Thus once again we will assay the Prince.
'T may be the sight of his own flesh and blood

Will

Emperour of Germany. 53

Will now at last pierce his obdurate heart.
Jailor how fares it with thy prisoner?
Let him appear upon the battlements.

 Hede. O mein deere vatter, ich habe in dis lang lang 30. weeken, welche mich duncket sein 40. jahr gewesen, ein litte Englisch gelernet, vnd ich hope, he will me verstohn, vnd shew me a litte pittie.

 Enter Edward *on the Walls and Jailor.*

 Saxon. Good morrow to your grace *Edward* of *Wales,*
Son and immediate Heir to *Henry* the third,
King of *England* and Lord of *Ireland,*
Thy Fathers comfort, and the peoples hope;
Tis not in mockage nor at unawares,
That I am ceremonious to repeat
Thy high descent joynd with thy Kingly might ;
But therewithall to intimate unto thee
What God expecteth from the higher powers,
Justice, and mercie, truth, sobrietie,
Relenting hearts, hands innocent of blood.
Princes are Gods chief substitutes on earth,
And shou'd be Lamps unto the common sort.
But you will say I am become a Preacher,
No, Prince, I am an humble suppliant,
And to prepare thine ears make this exordium,
To pierce thine eyes and heart, behold this spectacle.
Three Generations of the *Saxon* blood,
Descended lineallie from forth my Loyns,
Kneeling and crying to thy mightiness;
First look on me, and think what I have been,
For now I think my self of no account,
Next *Cæsar*, greatest man in *Germanie*,
Neerly a lyed, and ever friend to *England* ;
But Womens sighs move more in manly hearts,
O see the hands she elevates to Heaven,
Behold those eyes that whilome were thy joyes,
Uttering domb eloquence in Christal tears ;
If these exclames and sights be ordinarie,
Then look with pittie on thy other self,
This is thy flesh, and blood, bone of thy bone,

H 3

A goodly Boy the Image of his fire.
Turn'ſt thou away? O were thy Father here,
He would, as I do, take him in his arms,
And ſweetly kiſs his Grand-child in the face.
O *Edward* too young in experience,
That canſt not look into the grievous wrack,
Enſuing this thy obſtinate deniall;
O *Edward* too young in experience,
That canſt not ſee into the future good,
Enſuing thy moſt juſt acknowledgement;
Hear me thy trueſt friend, I will repeat them;
For good thou haſt an Heir indubitate,
Whoſe eyes a'ready ſparckle Majeſty,
Born in true Wedlock of a Princely Mother,
And all the *German* Princes to thy friends;
Where on the contrary thine eyes ſhall ſee,
The ſpeedy Tragedie of thee and thine;
Like *Athamas* firſt will I ceize upon
Thy young unchriſtened and deſpiſed Son,
And with his guiltleſs brains bepaint the Stones;
Then like *Virginius* will I kill my Child,
Unto thine eyes a pleaſing ſpectacle;
Yet ſhall it be a momentarie pleaſure,
Henry of *England* ſhall mourn with me;
For thou thy ſelf *Edward* ſhall make the third,
And be an actor in this bloody Scean.

   Hede. Ӝh mpne ſeete Edouart, mein herzkin, mpne ſcherzkin, mein herziges, einiges herz, mein allerleibeſt husband, I pzedee mein leeſe ſee me friendlich one, good ſeete harte tell de trut: and at leſt to me, and dpne allerleefeſt ſchild ſhew pitty I dan ich bin dpne, vnd dow biſt mpne, dow haſt me geben ein kindelein; O Edouart, ſeete, Edouart erbarmet ſein!

   Edw. O Hedewick peace, thy ſpeeches pierce my ſoul.

   Hede. Hedewick doe pow excellencie hight me Hedewick ſeete Edouart pow ſweete ich bin powr allerlieueſte wife.

   Edward. The Prieſt I muſt confeſs made thee my Wife,
Curſt be the damned villanous adulterer,
That with ſo fowl a blot divorc'd our love.

   Hede. O mein allerliebeſter, hiebozne Furſt vnd Herr,

Emperour of Germany.   55

dinck dat unser Herr Gott sitts in himmells trone, and sees
dat hart, vnd will my cause woll recken:

  Saxon. Edward hold me not up with long delays;
But quickly say, wilt thou confess the truth?
  Edward. As true as I am born of Kingly Linage,
And am the best *Plantagenet* next my Father,
I never carnallie did touch her body.
  Saxon. Edward this answer had we long ago,
Seest thou this brat? speak quickly or he dyes.
  Edward. His death will be more piercing to thine eyes,
Than unto mine, he is not of my kin.
  Hede. O Father, O myne Vatter spare myne kindt
O Edouart O Prince Edouart spreak now oder nimmer-
mehr, die kindt ist mein, it soll nicht sterben:
  Saxon. Have I dishonoured my self so much,
To bow my Knee to thee, which never bow'd
But to my God, and am I thus rewarded!
Is he not thine? speak murderous-minded Prince.
  Edward. O *Saxon, Saxon* mitigate thy rage.
First thy exceeding great humilitie,
When to thy captive prisoner thou didst kneel,
Had almost made my lying tongue confess,
The deed which I protest I never did;
But thy not causeless furious madding humour,
Together with thy Daughters pitious cryes,
Whom as my life and soul I dearly love,
Had thorowly almost perswaded me,
To save her honour and belie my self,
And were I not a Prince of so high blood,
And Bastards have no scepter-bearing hands,
I would in silence smother up this blot,
And in compassion of thy Daughters wrong,
Be counted Father to an others Child;
For why my soul knows her unguiltiness.
  Saxon. Smooth words in bitter sense; is thine answer?
  Hede. Ey vatter gene mir mein kindt, die kind ist mein.
  Saxon. Das weis ich woll, er sagt es ist nicht sein; there-
fore it dyes.   *He dashes out the Childs brains.*
  Hede. O Got in seinem trone, O mein kindt mein kindt.
  Saxon. There murderer take his head, and breathless lymbs,

Ther's

Ther's flesh enough, bury it in thy bowels,
Eat that, or dye for hunger, I protest,
Thou getst no other food till that be spent.
And now to thee lewd Whore, dishonour'd strumpet,
Thy turn is next, therefore prepare to dye.

   Edward. O mighty Duke of *Saxon*, spare thy Child.

   Sax. She is thy Wife *Edward*, and thou shouldst spare her,
One Gracious word of thine will save her life.

   Edward. I do confess *Saxon* she is mine own,
As I have marryed her, I will live with her,
Comfort thy self sweet *Hedewick* and sweet Wife.

   Hede. Ach, ach vnd wehe. warumb sagt your Excellence
nicht so before, now ist to late, vnser arme kindt ist kilt.

   Edward. Though thou be mine, and I do pittie thee,
I would not Nurse a Bastard for a Son.

   Hede. O Edouard now ich mark your mening ich sholdt
be your whore, mein Vatter ich begehr upon meine knee, las
mich lieber sterben, ade false Edouart, false Prince, ich be-
gehrs nicht.

   Saxon. Unprincely thoughts do hammer in thy head,
I'st not enough that thou hast sham'd her once,
And seen the Bastard torn before thy face;
But thou wouldst get more brats for Butcherie?
No *Hedewick* thou shalt not live the day.

   Hede. O Herr Gott, nimb meine seele in deiner henden.

   Saxon. It is thy hand that gives this deadly stroak.

   Hede. O Herr Sabote, das mein vnschuldt an tag kom-
men mocht.

   Edward. Her blood be on that wretched villains head,
That is the cause of all this misery.

   Saxon. Now murderous-minded Prince, hast thou beheld
Vpon my Child, and Childs Child, thy desire,
Swear to thy self, that here I firmly swear,
That thou shall surely follow her to morrow,
In Company of thy adulterous Aunt,
Jaylor convey him to his Dungeon,
If he be hungrie, I have thrown him meat,
If thirstie let him suck the newly born lymbs.

                                                    Edward.

Edward. O Heavens and Heavenly powers, if you be just,
Reward the author of this wickedness. *Exit. Edw. & Jaoler.*

Enter Alexander.

Alex. To arms great Duke of *Saxonie*, to arms,
My Lord of *Collen*, and the Earl of *Cornwall*,
In rescue of Prince *Edward* and the Empress,
Have levy'd fresh supplies, and presently
Will bid you battail in the open Field.

Sax. They never could have come in fitter time;
Thirst they for blood? and they shall quench their thirst.

Alex. O piteous spectacle! poor Princess *Hedewick*.

Sax. Stand not to pittie, lend a helping hand.

Alex. What slave hath murdered this guiltless Child?

Sax. What? dar'st thou call me slave unto my face?
I tell thee villain, I have done this deed,
And seeing the Father and the Grand sires heart,
Can give consent and execute their own,
Wherefore should such a rascal as thy self
Presume to pittie them, whom we have slain?

Alex. Pardon me, if it be presumption
To pittie them, I will presume no more.

Sax. Then help, I long to be amidst my foes.   *Exeunt.*

Alarum and Retreat.   **ACT. V.**

Enter Richard and Collen *with Drums and Souldiers.*

Richard. What means your Excellence to sound retreat?
This is the day of doom unto our Friend;
Before Sun set, my Sister, and my Nephew,
Vnless we rescue them, must lose their lives;
The cause admits no dalliance nor delay.
He that so tyrant-like hath slain his own,
Will take no pittie on a strangers blood.

Collen. At my entreaty e're we strike the battail,
Let's summon out our enemies to a parle.
Words spoken in time, have vertue, power, and price,

I   And

And mildneſs may prevail and take effect,
When dynt of Sword perhaps will aggravate.
  Rich. Then ſound a Parly to fulfill your mind,
Although I know no good can follow it.   *A Parley.*

  Enter Alphonſo, *Empreſs,* Saxon, Edward *priſoner,* Tryer,
    Brandenburg, Alexander *and Souldiers.*

  Alphon. Why how now Emperour that ſhould have been,
Are theſe the Engliſh Generals bravado's?
Make you aſſault ſo hotly at the firſt,
And in the ſelf ſame moment ſound retreat?
To let you know, that neither War nor words,
Have power for to divert their fatall doom,
Thus are we both reſolv'd; if we tryumph,
And by the right and juſtice of our cauſe
Obtain the victorie, as I doubt it not,
Then both of you ſhall bear them Company,
And e're Sun ſet we will perform our oaths,
With juſt effuſion of their guilty bloods;
If you be Conquerours, and we overcome,
Carry not that conceit to reſcue them,
My ſelf will be the Executioner,
And with theſe Ponyards fruſtrate all your hopes,
Making you tryumph in a bloodie Field.
  Saxon. To put you out of doubt that we intend it,
Pleaſe it your Majeſty to take your Seate,
And make a demonſtration of your meaning.
  Alphon. Firſt on my right hand bind the Engliſh Whore,
That venemous Serpent nurtt within my breaſt
To ſuck the vitall bloud out of my veins,
My Empreſs muſt have ſome preheminence,
Eſpecially at ſuch a bloodie Banquet,
Her State, and love to me deſerves no leſs.
  Saxon. That to Prince *Edward* I may ſhew my love,
And do the lateſt honour to his State,
Theſe hands of mine that never chained any,
Shall faſten him in fetters to the Chair.
Now Princes are you ready for the battail?
  Collen. Now att thou right the picture of thy ſelf
Seated in height of all thy Tyrannie;

But

But tell us what intends this spectacle.

Alphon. To make the certaintie of their deaths more plain,
And Cancel all your hopes to save their lives,
While *Saxon* leads the troups into the Field,
Thus will I vex their souls, with sight of death,
Loudly exclaming in their half dead ears;
That if we win they shall have companie,
Viz. The English Emperour,
And you my Lord Archbishop of *Collen*,
If we be vanquisht, then they must expect
Speedy dispatch from these two Daggers points.

Collen. What canst thou tyrant then expect but death?

Alphon. Tush hear me out, that hand which shed their blood,
Can do the like to rid me out of bonds.

Rich. But that's a damned resolution.

Alphon. So must this desperate disease be cur'd.

Rich. O *Saxon* I'le yield my self and all my power,
To save my Nephew, though my Sister dye.

Sax. Thy Brothers Kingdom shall not save his life.

Edward. Uncle, you see these savage minded men
Will have no other ransome but my blood,
England hath Heirs, though I be never King,
And hearts and hands to scourge this tyrannie,
And so farewel.

Emp. A thousand times farewel,
Sweet Brother *Richard* and brave Prince of *Collen*.

Sax. What *Richard*, hath this object pierc'd thy heart?
By this imagine how it went with me,
When yesterday I slew my Children.

Rich. O *Saxon* I entreat thee on my Knees.

Sax. Thou shalt obtain like mercy with thy kneeling,
As lately I obtaind at *Edward*'s hands.

Rich. Pitty the tears I powr before thy feet.

Sax. Pitty those tears? why I shed bloudie tears.

Rich. I'le do the like to save Prince *Edwards* life.

Sax. Then like a Warrior spill it in the Field,
My griefull anger cannot be appeaz'd,
By sacrifice of any but himself,
Thou hast dishonour'd me, and thou shalt dye;

I 2   Therefore

Therefore alarum, alarum to the fight,
That thousands more may bear thee company.
 Rich. Nephew and Sister. now farewell for ever.
 Ed. Heaven and the Right prevail, and let me die;
Uncle farewell.
 Emp. Brother farewell untill wee meet in Heaven.
   Exeunt. Manent A phon. Edw. Emp. Alex.
 Alphon. Here's farewell Brother, Nephew, Vncle, Aunt,
As if in thousand years you should not meet;
Good Nephew, and good Aunt content your selves,
The Sword of *Saxon* and these Daggers-points,
Before the Evening-Star doth shew it self,
Will take sufficient order for your meeting.
But *Alexander*, my trustie *Alexander*,
Run to the Watch-Tow'r as I pointed thee,
And by thy life I charge thee look unto it
Thou be the first to bring me certain word
I we be Conquerors, or Conquered.
 Alex. With carefull speed I will perform this charge. *Exit.*
 Alphon Now have I leasure yet to talk with you.
Fair *Isabell*, the *Palsgrave's* Paramour,
Wherein was he a better man than I?
Or wherfore should thy love to him, effect
Such deadly hate unto thy Emperour?
Yet welfare wenches that can love Good fellows
And not mix Murder with Adulterie.
 Emp. Great Emperor, I dare not call you Husband,
Your Conscience knows my hearts unguiltinefs.
 Alpho. Didst thou not poison, or consent to poison us?
 Emp. Should any but your Highness tell me so,
I should forget my patience at my death,
And call him Villain, Liar, Murderer.
 Alphon. She that doth so miscall me at her end,
Edward I prethee speak thy Conscience,
Thinkst thou not that in her prosperitie
Sh'hath vext my Soul with bitter Words and Deeds?
O Prince of *England* I do count thee wife
That thou wilt not be cumber'd with a wife,
When thou hadst stoln her daintie rose Corance,
And pluck'd the flow'r of her virginitie.

            Edw.

Edw. Tyrant of *Spain* thou liest in thy throat.
Alpho. Good words, thou seest thy life is in our hands.
Edw. I see thou art become a common Hangman,
An Office farre more fitting to thy mind
Than princelie to the Imperiall dignitie.
Alphon. I do not exercise on common persons,
Your Highness is a Prince, and she an Empress,
I therefore count not of a dignitie.
Hark *Edward* how they labour all in vain,
With loss of many a valiant Soldiers life,
To rescue them whom Heaven and we have doom'd;
Dost thou not tremble when thou think'st upon't?
Edw. Let guiltie minds tremble at sight of Death.
My heart is of the nature of the Palm,
Not to be broken, till the highest Bud
Be bent and ti'd unto the lowest Root;
I rather wonder that thy Tyrants heart
Can give content that those thy Butcherous hands
Should offer violence to thy Flesh and Blood.
See how her guiltless innocence doth plead
In silent Oratorie of her chastest tears.
Alphon. Those tears proceed from Fury and curst heart.
I know the stomach of your English Dames.
Emp. No Emperour, these tears proceed from grief.
Alphon. Grief that thou canst not be reveng'd of Vs.
Emp. Grief that your Highness is so ill advis'd,
To offer violence to my Nephew *Edward*;
Since then there must be sacrifice of Blood,
Let my heart-blood save both your bloods unspilt,
For of his death, thy Heart must pay the guilt.
Edw. No Aunt, I will not buy my life so dear:
Therefore *Alphonso* if thou beest a man
Shed manly blood, and let me end this strife.
Alphon. Here's straining curt'sie at a bitter Feast.
Content thee Empress for thou art my Wife,
Thou shalt obtain thy Boon and die the death,
And for it were unprinceby to deny
So slight request unto so great a Lord,
Edward shall bear thee company in Death.   *A Retreat.*
But hark the heat of battail hath an end;

One

One side or other hath the victory,   *Enter Alexander.*
And see where *Alexander* sweating comes;
Speak man, what newes. speak, shall I die or live?
Shall I stab sure, or els prolong their lives
To grievous Torments? speak, am I Conquerour?
What, hath thy hast bereft thee of thy speech?
Hast thou not breath to speak one sillable?
O speak, thy dalliance kills me, wonn or lost?   *Amaz'd*
  Alex. Lost.   *lets fall the*
   Alphon. Ah me my Senses fail! my sight is gon. *Daggers.*
   Alex. Will not your Grace dispatch the Strumpet Queen?
Shall she then live, and we be doom'd to death?
Is your Heart faint, or is your Hand too weak?
Shall servill fear break your so sacred Oaths?
Me thinks an Emperour should hold his word;
Give me the Weapons, I will soon dispatch them,
My Fathers yelling Ghost cries for revenge,
His Blood within my Veins boyls for revenge;
O give me leave *Cesar* to take revenge.
   Alphon. Vpon condition that thou wilt protest
To take revenge upon the Murtherers,
Without respect of dignity, or State,
Afflicted, speedy, pittiless Revenge,
I will commit this Dagger to thy trust,
And give thee leave to execute thy Will.
   Alex. What need I here reiterate the Deeds
Which deadly sorrow made me perpetrate?
How neer did I entrap Prince *Richard's* life?
How sure set I the Knife to *Mentz* his heart?
How cunninglie was *Palsgrave* doom'd to death?
How subtilly was *Bohem* poisoned?
How slily did I satisfie my lust
Commixing dulcet Love with deadly Hate,
When Princesse *Hedwick* lost her Maidenhead,
Sweetly embracing me for *Englands* Heir?
  Edw. O execrable deeds!
  Emp. O salvage mind!
  Alex. Edward, I give thee leave to hear of this,
But will forbid the blabbing of your tongue.
Now gratious Lord and sacred Emperour,   *Your*

Your highnefs knowing thefe and many more,
Which fearles pregnancie hath wrought in me,
You do me wrong to doubt that I will dive
Into their hearts that have not fpar'd their betters,
Be therefore fuddain left we die our felves.
I know the Conquerour hafts to refcue them.

Alphon. Thy Reafons are effectuall, take this Dagger;
Yet pawfe a while.

Emp. Sweet Nephew now farewell.

Alphon. They are moft dear to me whom thou muft kill.

Edward. Hark Aunt he now begins to pittie you.

Alex. But they confented to my Fathers death.

Alphon. More then confented, they did execute.

Emp. I will not make his Majeftie a Lyar,
I kil. d thy Father, therefore let me die,
But fave the life of this unguilty Prince.

Edward. I kill'd thy Father, therefore let me die,
But ave the life of this unguiltie Emprefs.

Alphon Hark thou to me, and think their words as wind
I kill'd thy Father, therfore let me die,
And fave the lives of thefe two guiltlefs Princes.
Art thou amaz'd to hear what I have faid?
There, take the weapon, now revenge at full
Thy Fathers death, and thofe my dire deceits
That made thee murtherer of fo many Souls.

Alex. O Emperour, how cunningly wouldft thou entrap
My fimple youth to credit Fictions?
Thou kill my Father, no, no Emperour,
Cæfar did love *Lorenzo* all to dearly:
Seeing thy Forces now are vanquifhed,
Fruftrate thy hopes, thy Highnefs like to fall
Into the cruel and revengefull hands
Of mercilefs incenfed Enemies,
Like *Caius Caffius* wearie of thy life,
Now wouldft thou make thy Page an inftrument
By fuddain ftroak to rid thee of thy bonds.

Alphon. Haft thou forgotten how that very night
Thy Father dy'd, I took the Mafter-Key,
And with a lighted Torch walk'd through the Court.

Alex. I muft remember that, for to my death

I never shall forget the slightest deed,
Which on that dismall Night or Day I did.

   Alphon. Thou wast no sooner in thy restfull Bed,
But I disturb'd thy Father of his rest,
And to be short, not that I hated him,
But for he knew my deepest Secrets,
With cunning Poison I did end his life:
Art thou his Son? express it with a Stabb,
And make account if I had prospered,
Thy date was out, thou wast already doom'd,
Thou knewst too much of me to live with me.

   Alex. What wonders do I hear great Emperour?
Not that I do stedfastlie believe
That thou didst murder my beloved Father;
But in meer pittie of thy vanquish'd state
I undertake this execution.
Yet, for I fear the sparkling Majestie.
Which issues from thy most Imperial, eyes
May strike relenting Passion to my heart,
And after wound receiv'd from fainting hand,
Thou fall halfe dead among thine Enemies,
I crave thy Highness leave to bind thee first.

   Alphon. Then bind me quickly, use me as thou please
   Emp. O Villain, wilt thou kill thy Sovereign?
   Alex. Your Highness sees that I am forc'd unto it.
   Alphon. Fair Empress, I shame to ask thee pardon,
Whom I have wrong'd so many thousand waies.

   Emp. Dread Lord and Husband, leave these desperat
Doubt not the Princes may be reconcil'd.   (thoughts,

   Alex. 'T may be the Princes will be reconcil'd,
But what is that to me? all Potentates on Earth
Can never reconcile my grieved Soul.
Thou slew'st my Father, thou didst make this hand
Mad with Revenge to murther Innocents,
Now hear, how in the height of all thy pride
The rightfull Gods have powr'd their justfull wrath
Upon thy Tyrants head, Devill as thou art,
And sav'd by miracle these Princes lives;
For know, thy side hath got the Victory;
Saxon triumphs over his dearest friends;

                                      Richard

Richard and *Collen*, both are Prisoners,
And every thing hath forted to thy wish;
Only hath Heaven put it in my mind
(for he alone directed then my thoughts
Although my meaning was most mischievous)
To tell thee thou hadst lost, in certain hope
That suddainly thou wouldst have slain them both,
For if the Princes came to talk about it,
I greatly feard their lives might be prolong'd.
Art thou not mad to think on this deceit?
Ile make thee madder, with tormenting thee.
I tell thee Arch-Thief, Villain, Murtherer,
Thy Forces have obtaind the Victory,
Victory leads thy Foes in captive bands;
This Victory hath crown'd thee Emperour,
Only my self have vanquisht Victory,
And triumph in the Victors overthrow.

 Alphon. O *Alexander* spare thy Princes life.
 Alex. Even now thou didst entreat the contrary.
 Alphon. Think what I am that begg my life of thee.
 Alex. Think what he was whom thou hast doom'd to death.
But least the Princes do surprize us here
Before I have perform'd my strange revenge,
I will be suddain in the execution.
 Alphon. I will accept any condition.
 Alex. Then in the presence of the Emperess,
The captive Prince of *England*, and my self,
Forswear the joyes of Heaven, the fight of God,
Thy Souls salvation, and thy Saviour Christ,
Damning thy Soul to endless pains of Hell.
Do this or die upon my Rapiers point.
 Emp. Sweet Lord and Husband, spit in's face,
Die like a man, and live not like a Devill.
 Alex. What? wilt thou save thy life, and damn thy Soul?
 Alph. O hold thy hand, *Alphonsus* doth renounce.
 Edward. Aunt stop your years, hear not this Blasphemy.
 Empr. Sweet Husband think that Christ did dy for thee.
 Alphon. Alphonsus doth renounce the joyes of Heaven,
The fight of Angells and his Saviours blood,
And gives his Soul unto the Devills power.
 Alex. Thus will I make delivery of the Deed.

     K   Dye

ALPHONSUS

Die and be damn'd now am I satisfied.
  Edward. O damned Miscreant, what hast thou done?
  Alex. When I have leasure I will answer thee:
Mean while I'le take my heels and save my self.
If I be ever call'd in question,
I hope your Majesties will save my life,
You have so happily preserved yours;
Did I not think it, both of you should die.   *Exit Alex.*

   Enter Saxon, Branden. Tryer, *(* Richard *and* Collen
     as prisoners) and Soldiers.

  Saxon. Bring forth these daring Champions to the Block,
Comfort your selves you shall have company.
Great Emperor, where is his Majestie?
What bloody spectacle do I behold?
  Emp. Revenge, revenge O *Saxon, Brandenburg,*
My Lord is slain, *Cæsar* is doom'd to death.
  Edward. Princes make haste, follow the murtherer
  Saxon. Is *Cæsar* slain?
  Edward Follow the Murtherer.
  Emp. Why stand you gasing on an other thus?
Follow the Murtherer.
  Saxon. What Murtherer?
  Edward. The villain *Alexander* hath slain his Lord,
Make after him with speed, so shall you hear
Such vilanie as you have never heard.
  Brand. My Lord of *Tryer,* we both with our light Horse
Will scoure the Coasts and quickly bring him in.
  Saxon. That can your Excellence alone perform,
Stay you my Lord, and guard the Prisoners,
While I, alas, unhappiest Prince alive,
Over his Trunk consume my self in Tears.
Hath *Alexander* done this damned deed?
That cannot be why sheu'd he slay his Lord?
O cruel Fate, O miserable me!
Me thinks I now present *Mark Antony,*
Folding dead *Julius Cæsar* in mine arms.
No, no, I rather will present *Achilles,*
And on *Patroclus* Tomb do sacrifice.

                                          Let

Emperour of Germany.

Let me be spurn'd and hated as a Dogg,
But I perform more direfull bloody Rites
Than *Thetis* Son for *Menetiades.*
  Edward. Leave mourning for thy Foes, pitty thy Friends.
  Sax. Friends have I none, and that which grieves my Soul,
Is want of Foes to work my wreak upon;
But were you Traitors 4, four hundred thousand,
Then might I satisfie my self with Blood.

    Enter Brandenb. Alexand. *and Soldiers.*

  Saxon. See *Alexander* where *Cæsar* lieth slain,
The guilt whereof the Traitors call on thee;
Speak, canst thou tell who slew thy Soveraign?
  Alexan. Why who but I? how should I curse my self
If any but my self had done this deed?
This happy hand, blest be my hand therefore,
Reveng'd my Fathers death upon his Soul:
And *Saxon* thou hast cause to curse and bann
That he is dead, before thou didst inflict
Torments on him that so hath torn thy heart.
  Saxon. What Mysteries are these?
  Bran. Princes, can you inform us of the Truth?
  Edward. The Deed's so heinous that my faltering tongue
Abhorres the utterance. Yet I must tell it.
  Alex. Your Highness shall not need to take the pains,
What you abhorr to tell, I joy to tell,
Therefore be silent and give audience.
You mighty men, and Rulers of the Earth,
Prepare your Ears, to hear of Stratagems
Whose dire effects have gaul'd your princely hearts,
Confounded your conceits, muffled your eyes:
First to begin, this villanous Fiend of Hell
Murther'd my Father, sleeping in his Chair,
The reason why, because he only knew
All Plots, and complots of his villanie;
His death was made the Basis and the Ground
Of every mischief that hath troubled you.
  Saxon. If thou, thy Father and thy Progenie
Were hang'd and burnt, and broken on the Wheel

K 2   How

How could their deaths heap mischief on our heads?
  Alex. And if you will not hear the Reason chuse.
I tell thee I have slain an Emperour,
And thereby think my self as good a man
As thou, or any man in Christendom;
Thou shalt entreat me ere I tell thee more.
  Brand. Proceed
  Alex. Not I.
  Saxon I prethe now proceed.
  Alex. Since you intreat me then, I will proceed.
This murtherous Devill having slain my Father,
Buz'd cunningly into my credulous ears,
That by a General Councell of the States,
And as it were by Act of Parlement,
The seven Electors had set down his death,
And made the Empress Executioner,
Transferring all the guilt from him to you.
This I believ'd, and first did set upon
The life of Princely *Richard*, by the Boors,
But how my purpose faild in that, his Grace best knows;
Next, by a double intricate deceit,
Midst all his Mirth was *Bohem* poysoned,
And good old *Mentz* to save *Alphonso*'s life.
(Who at that instant was in perfect health)
Twixt jest and earnest was made a Sacrifice;
As for the *Palatine*, your Graces knew
His Highness and the Queens unguiltines;
But now my Lord of *Saxon* hark to me,
Father of *Saxon* should I rather call you,
Twas I that made your Grace a Grandfather:
Prince *Edward* plow'd the ground, I sow'd the Seed,
Pour *Hedewick* bore the most unhappy fruit,
Created in a most unluckie hour,
To a most violent and untimely death.
  Sax. O loathsome Villain, O detested deeds,
O guiltless Prince, O me most miserable.
  Brand. But tell us who reveal'd to thee at last
This shamefull guilt, and our unguiltiness?
  Alex. Why that's the wonder Lords, and thus it was:
When like a tyrant he had tane his seat,

                             And

Emperour of Germany.

And that the furie of the Fight began,
Upon the highest Watch-Tow'r of the Fort,
It was my office to behold alofft
The Warres event, and having seen the end,
I saw how Victory with equal wings
Hang hovering 'twixt the Battails here and there,
Till at the last, the English Lyons fled,
And *Saxon*'s side obtain'd the Victory;
Which seen, I posted from the turrets top,
More furiously than ere *Laocoon* ran,
When Trojan hands drew in *Troy's* overthrow,
But yet as fatally as he or any.
The tyrant seeing me, star'd in my face,
And suddainly demanded whats the newes,
I, as the Fates would have it, hoping that he
Even in a twinkling would have slain 'em both,
For so he swore before the Fight began,
Cri'd bitterly that he had lost the day,
The sound whereof did kill his dastard heart,
And made the Villain desperatly confess
The murther of my Father, praying me,
With dire revenge, to ridd him of his life;
Short tale to make, I bound him cunningly,
Told him of the deceit, triumphing over him,
And lastly with my Rapier slew him dead.

  Sax. O Heavens! justly have you tane revenge.
But thou, thou murtherous adulterous slave,
What Bull of *Phalaris*, what strange device,
Shall we invent to take away thy life?

  Alex. If *Edward* and the Empress, whom I sav'd,
Will not requite it now, and save my life,
Then let me die, contentedly I die,
Having at last reveng'd my Fathers death.

  Sax. Villain, not all the world shall save thy life.

  Edw. Hadst thou not been Author of my *Hedewicks* death,
I would have certainly sav'd thee from death;
But if my Sentence now may take effect,
I would adjudge the Villain to be hang'd
As here the Jewes are hang'd in *Germany*.

  Sax. Young Prince it shall be so; go dragg the Slave

K 3   Unto

Unto the place of execution:
There let the *Judas*, on a jewish Gallowes,
Hang by the heels between two English Mastives,
There feed on Doggs, let Doggs there feed on thee,
And by all means prolong his miserie.

    Alex. O might thy self and all these English Currs,
Instead of Mastive-Doggs hang by my side,
How sweetly would I tugg upon your Flesh.   *Exit Alex.*

    Sax. Away with him, suffer him not to speak.
And now my lords, *Collen, Tryer,* and *Barndenburg,*
Whose Hearts are bruz'd to think upon these woes,
Though no man hath such reason as my self,
We of the seven Electors that remain,
After so many bloody Massacres,
Kneeling npon our Knees, humbly intreat,
Your Excellence to be our Emperour.
The Royalties of the Coronation
Shall be at *Aix,* shortly solemnized.

    Cullen. Brave Princely *Richard* now refuse it not,
Though the Election be made in Tears,
Joy shall attend thy Coronation.

    Richard. It stands not with mine Honour to deny it,
Yet by mine honour, fain I would refuse it.

    Edward. Uncle, the weight of all these Miseries
Maketh my heart as heavy as your own,
But an Imperial Crown would lighten it.
Let this one reason make you take the Crown.

    Richard. What's that sweet nephew?

    Edward. Sweet Uncle, this it is,
Was never Englishman yet Emperour,
Therefore to honour *England* and your self,
Let private sorrow yield to publike Fame,
That once an Englishman bare *Cæsar*'s name.

    Richard. Nephew, thou hast prevail'd; Princes stand up,
We humbly do accept your sacred offer.

    Cullen. Then sound the Trumpets, and cry *Vivat Cæsar.*

    All. Vivat Cæsar.

    Cullen. Richardus Dei gratia Romanorum Imperator, semper Augustus, Comes Cornubiæ.

    Richard

Richard. Sweet Sister now let *Cæsar* comfort you,
And all the rest that yet are comfortless;
Let them expect from English *Cæsar's* hands
Peace, and abundance of all earthly Joy.

FINIS

Notes

NOTES

Page 1

Stage direction: Alexander de Tripes.
This character is later referred to as Alexander de Toledo, and his father, who in the *dramatis personæ* appears as *Lorenzo de Cipres* (a probable misprint for Cyprus), is on p. 13, l. 4, spoken of as *Lorenzo de Toledo*.

Page 2

Line 15: He learns his wisdom, not by flight of Birds.
Compare with *Æneid*, Bk. III, ll. 359–361:

> "*Trōiugena, interpres dīvum, qui nūmina Phœbī,
> quī tripodas, Clarii laurūs, quī sidera sentīs
> et volucrum linguās et præpetis ōmina pinnæ,*" etc.

Line 16: By prying into sacrificed beasts.
Compare this passage with *Æneid*, Bk. IV, ll. 63–64:

> "*. . . pecudumque reclusis
> pectoribus inhians spirantia consulit exta.*"

Line 17: By Hares that cross the way.
Compare with Webster's *Duchess of Malfi*, Act II, sc. 2:

> "The throwing down salt, or *crossing of a hare*
> . . . are of power
> To daunt whole man in us."

Line 17: by howling Wolves.

Alphonsus

The wolf had an uncanny reputation among the Elizabethans. Thus in *Macbeth*, Act II, sc. 1, appear the lines:

" . . . and wither'd Murther
Alarum'd by his centinell, the Wolfe
Whose howle's his Watch," etc.

Duchess of Malfi, Act IV, sc. 1:

"The wolf shall find her grave, and scrape it up,
Not to devour the corpse, but to discover
The horrid murder."

Also see *God's Revenge against Murther*, Bk. VI, Hist. 27, p. 407, ed. 1670.

Page 3

Line 1: Una arbusta non alit duos Erithicos:—
"οὐ τρέφει μία λόχμη δύο ἐριθάκους" *Schol. Aristoph. Vesp.*, 922. *Stephani Thesaur. s.* Ἐρίθακος. *Plin. Hist. Nat.*, x, 29, 44 [Elze's note].

Line 41: I. A Prince must be of the nature of the Lion and the Fox; but not the one without the other.

Meyer points out (*Machiavelli and the Elizabethan Drama*, pp. 134–135) that this maxim is derived from Gentillet's *Discours sur les Moyens de bien gouverner et maintenir en bonne paix un Royaume ou autre Principauté . . . Contre Nicholas Machiavel*, 1576, popularly known as *Contre Machiavel*.

Meyer gives, for purposes of comparison, the passage from *Il Principe*, followed by the derived passage in *Contre Machiavel* and the corresponding passage in Patericke's rendering of Gentillet.

Machiavelli (chap. xviii) says: "*Essendo adunque un principe necessitato sapere bene usare la bestia, debbe di quella pigliare la volpe ed il leone; perchè il leone non si difende dai lacci, la volpe non si difende da' lupi. Bisogna adunque essere volpe a conoscere i lacci, e lione a sbigottire i lupi. Coloro che stanno semplicemente in sul lione non se ne intendono."*

Gentillet's version reads: *"Le Prince doit ensuyure la nature du Lyon, et du Renard: non de l'un sans l'autre."*

Patericke translates: "A prince ought to follow the nature of the Lyon and of the Fox, yet not of the one without the other."

Page 4

Lines 3–6: I'l imitate *Lysander* in this point,
And where the Lion's hide is thin and scant,
I'l firmly patch it with the Foxes fell.
Let it suffice I can be both in one.

Compare this passage with Plutarch's *Lysander*, which would seem to be its source: "When he [Lysander] was told, it did not become the descendants of Hercules to adopt such artful expedients, he turned it off with a jest, and said, 'Where the lion's skin falls short, it must be eked out with the fox's.'"

Also compare with lines 1732–4 in *Selimus:*

"I like Lysander's counsel passing well;
'If that I cannot speed with lion's force
To clothe my complots in a fox's skin.'"

It is a singular coincidence that both this passage from *Selimus* and the one from *Alphonsus* are imbedded in material Machiavellian in character.

Lines 7–9: 2. A Prince above all things must seem devout; but there is nothing so dangerous to his state, as to regard his promise or his oath.

For this passage Meyer (p. 135) refers the reader to Gentillet, ii, 1, and iii, 21. The former reads: *"Un prince, sur toutes choses, doit appeter d'estre estimé devot, bien qu'il ne le soit pas."* The latter reads: *"Le Prince prudent ne doit observer la foy, quand l'observation luy en est dommageable, et que les occasions qui la luy ont fait promettre sont passees."* Meyer likewise makes reference to *Principe*, 18: *Discorsi*, iii, 42.

Lines 15–16: 3. Trust not a reconciled friend; for good turns cannot blot out old grudges.

Meyer (p. 135) directs the reader to Gentillet, iii, 6, a passage which is worded as follows: *"C'est folie de penser que nouveaux plaisirs facent oublier vieilles offences aux grands Seigneurs."* Reference is likewise made to *Principe*, 7: *Discorsi*, iii, 4: *Ist. Fior.*, iv (217).

Lines 25–32: This speech should be assigned to Lorenzo, not to Alphonsus.

Page 5

Line 1: Hungarian Ducates.

"The Gold Ducket of Hungary," says Fynes Moryson (*Itinerary*, vol. ii, p. 143), "is of the purest gold of twenty foure Caracts, and it is two penny weight and sixe graines . . . ; and in England they are worth seven shillings and two pence." On p. 124 of this volume Moryson states that this coin was in use in Bohemia, was most current in Vienna and the confines of Hungary, and was used more extensively than other large coins in Dantzic and throughout all Poland. Moryson goes on to say (vol. ii, pp. 154 and 158) that the Hungarian Ducat was of the same standard, fineness, and value as the Venetian zecchine and the Turkish Sultanon.

Line 1: Crusadoes.

According to Moryson (*Itinerary*, vol. ii, p. 145), "the short and long Crusado was esteemed at five and thirty, the Hungarian Ducket at thirty silver Groshen" [the silver grosh was worth more than twopence and less than twopence halfpenny English money]. This was the value in Magdeburg, Leipzig, Misen, in all the Electorate of Saxony, and in the neighbouring territories, to the confines of Bohemia.

Line 3: English Angels.

Fynes Moryson (*Itinerary*, vol. i, p. 23) gives the value of this coin: "A Gold Angell of the standard of 23 Caracts 3 graines and an halfe, is three peny waight and 8 graines, and is given for ten silver shillings, 12 pence making a shilling, the silver being of the standard of 11 ounces two peny weight, and the shilling foure penny (or ninety six graines) weight." This standard was adopted in the year 1600. The standard of the year 1609 was lighter than the standard of the year 1600 by ten pence in each angel, and the second standard of this same year was lighter in like proportion than the second standard of the year 1600. See Fynes Moryson, *Itinerary*, vol. ii, pp. 135-137. The facility with which the word angel lent itself to punning proved here, as in other instances throughout the Elizabethan drama, an irresistible temptation.

Line 4: crosses.

Pieces of money, so named because many pieces had a cross on one side.

Line 7: holiness.

Elze thus explains the application of this title to the Archbishop of Mentz: "From the times of St. Boniface the Archbishop of Mentz was always considered the highest dignitary of the Church next to the Pope; his was a Holy See (*heiliger Stuhl*) like the Pope's, whilst the other Archbishops were styled Archbishops of the Holy Cathedrals (*der heiligen Kirche*) of Collen, Trier, etc."

Lines 12-13: for in election his voice is first.

This is an error. Fynes Moryson, on the authority of the *Golden Bull*, gives the order of registering the choice as follows: It is decreed "that the Arch-bishop of Mentz shall aske the Voyces first, of the Arch-bishop of Trier, then of the Arch-bishop of Colon, then of the King of Bohemia, then of the Palatine, then of the Duke of Saxony, then of the Marquis of Brandeburg, and lastly that these Princes shall aske the Voyce of the Arch-bishop of Mentz" (*Itinerary*, vol. iv, p. 258).

Line 14: 4. 'T is more safety for a Prince to be feared than loved.

Meyer makes reference (*Machiavelli and the English Drama*, p. 136) to Gentillet, iii, 9. Also *Principe*, 17: *Discorsi*, iii, 21: *Ist. Fior.*, ii (130). Gentillet, iii, 9, reads: "*Mieux vaut à un Prince d'estre craint qu'aimé.*"

Lines 15–18: Love is an humour pleaseth him that loves;
Let me be hated, so I please my self.
Love is an humour mild and changeable;
But fear engraves a reverence in the heart."

Meyer (p. 136) calls attention to the fact that Gentillet says: "*Les hommes (dit nostre Florentin) aiment comme il leur plait, et craignent comme il plait au Prince,*" and that Machiavelli says: "*Concludo adunque, tornando all' esser temuto et amato, che amando gli uomini a posta loro, et temendo a posta del principe, deve un principe savio fondarsi in su quello che è suo, non in su quello che è d'altri.*" Meyer concludes from this that the author of *Alphonsus* had Gentillet and not Machiavelli before him.

Lines 19–22: 5. To keep an usurped Crown, a Prince must swear, forswear, poyson, murder, and commit all kind of villanies, provided it be cunningly kept from the eye of the world.

Meyer (p. 136) refers to Gentillet, iii, 18; also *Principe*, 18: *Discorsi*, ii, 13: *Ist. Fior.*, iii (147). Meyer further calls attention to the fact that in the reference to "poison, murder, and all kinds of villainies" the influence of Marlowe and the drama subsequent to Marlowe is apparent. The passage in Gentillet referred to reads: "*Le Prince ne doit craindre de se perjurer, tromper et dissimuler: car le trompeur trouve tousiours qui se laisse tromper.*"

Lines 31–34: 6. Be alwaies jealous of him that knows your secrets,
And therefore it behooves you credit few;
And when you grow into the least suspect,
With silent cunning must you cut them off.

"This last," says Meyer, p. 136, "is not to be found exactly as stated either in Machiavelli or Gentillet, but must have been perverted by the dramatists from *Principe*, 23."
See Introduction to this edition.

Line 40: That it is twenty days before it works.
See Introduction.

Page 6

Line 12: *Aeneas Pilot* by the God of dreams.
A reference to Palinurus. For an account of Palinurus' fatal sleep see the closing portion of Bk. V of the *Æneid*.

Page 7

Line 2: We the seven Pillars of the German Empire.
Elze calls attention to the fact that the Electors are referred to as pillars in *Bulla Aurea*, chap. xii: "*Sacri Imperii Electores . . . qui solidæ bases Imperii et columnæ immobiles*," which citation in the English edition of the *Golden Bull* (1619) reads: "Which sound pillers and stedfast and immoveable supporters of the Empire."

Line 9: Sewer to the Emperour.
This title is wrongly assigned to the King of Bohemia, belonging by rights to the Palatine. Fynes Moryson calls the King of Bohemia "Archbutler of the Empire" (*Itinerary*, vol. iv, p. 256).

Alphonsus

Line 10 *sqq.:* Do take my seat next to the sacred throne.
Elze points out that "the precedence here assigned to the Princes Electors does not agree with the *Golden Bull.*"

Line 12: Archbishop of *Mentz,* Chancelor of *Germany.*
In his *Crudities,* vol. ii, p. 275, Coryat states that the Archbishop of Mentz is "intituled Chancellor of Germany for the more addition of dignity." Moryson, too, alludes to the Archbishop under this title (*Itinerary,* vol. iv, p. 256).

Line 16: His Highness Taster.
Strictly not Taster but chief Sewer, an office which the author of *Alphonsus* wrongly assigns to the King of Bohemia. Coryat in his *Crudities,* vol. ii, p. 223, assigns the Palatine his full title, "*Serenissimus Princeps etc, Elector, Comes Palatinus ad Rhenum, Sacri Romani Imperii Archidapifer, et Bavariæ Dux.*" He is intituled *Archidapifer,* he explains (vol. ii, p. 224), "because he is chiefe Sewer to the Emperour, and attendeth him at Table the first meale that hee maketh after his Election, according to an ancient custome that hath beene continually observed at the Emperours election any time these six hundred yeares and a little more, by the first institution of Otho the third Germane Emperor of that name." Fynes Moryson confirms the statement regarding this custom (*Itinerary,* vol. iv, p. 256): "The Count Palatine of the Rheine carries the first dish at the feast of the Emp. coronation."

Line 26: Chancelor of *Gallia.*
Should be Chancellor of Italy.
Coryat (*Crudities,* vol. ii, p. 333) cites two epitaphs in which the titles of the Archbishops of Cologne appear:
"*Reverendissimo Domino D. Adolpho Archiepo. ac Principi Electori Coloniensi, S. Rom. Impii per Italiam Archicancellario, legatoque nato, Westphaliæ et Angariæ Duci,* etc. *ex illustri familiâ Comitum à Schawenburg oriundo,*" etc.
Another epitaph:
"*Reverendissimo Domino D. Antonio electo ac confirmato Principi Electori Coloniensi, S. S. Imperii Per Italiam*

Archcancellario, Legatoque nato, Westphaliæ e Angariæ Duci, ex illustri familiâ Comitum à Schawenburg oriundo," etc.

Moryson calls the Archbishop of Cologne "Chancelor for Italy" (*Itinerary*, vol. iv, p. 256).

Line 32: Arch-Marshal, to the Emperour.

Fynes Moryson refers to the Duke of Saxony as the "Marshal of the Empire" (*Itinerary*, vol. iv, p. 256).

Line 34: Chancelour of Italie.

This is the title of the Archbishop of Cologne. Trier was Chancellor of Gallia, an office wrongly assigned to Cologne.

Line 37: Whose Office is to be the Treasurer.

This was not the office of Brandenburg, who, on the contrary, was "Great Chamberlaine," under which title Fynes Moryson refers to him (*Itinerary*, vol. iv, p. 256).

Page 8

Line 33: when we once are set.

Elze has the following note on this passage:—

"I am unable to say, whether or not the custom alluded to in the text was really observed in the elective council; thus much, however, is certain, that it admirably harmonizes with the directions contained in the Golden Bull: 'They (viz. the Electors) shall proceed to the Election and shall not in any manner depart out of the said Citie of Franckford, before that the greater part of them shall have chosen a temporall head or governour of the world or of Christendome, a King of Romains, to be Emperour, which if they shall prolong or deferre the space of thirty dayes from the day of taking their oathes, then the said thirty dayes being expired, they shall eate nothing but bread and water, nor by any meanes goe away from the said Citie, untill or before they or the greater number of them shall have chosen the ruler or temporall head of Christendome, as aforesaid.' Compare also the following passage from *Römer-*

Büchner, Die Wahl und Krönung der deutschen Kaiser zu Frankfurt a. M. (Frankf. a. M., 1858), p. 34 sq.: 'Die Wahl-kapelle, Capella regia oder imperatoria, in der Bartholo-mäikirche [zu Frankfurt], welche wahrscheinlich Karl IV. selbst erbauen liess, befindet sich auf der Südseite des hohen Chores, ist 45 Fuss lang und 16 Fuss breit und hat nur Einen Eingang, nämlich vom hohen Chor aus, indem diejenige Thür, welche aus der Wahlkapelle in die Heilig-Grabkapelle führt, erst später gebrochen zu sein scheint. Auf der Süd-seite der Wahlkapelle finden wir seitwärts an den beiden mit-tleren Fenstern zwei zugemauerte Oeffnungen, die keine Thüren sein können. Wenn auch in späteren Zeiten und namentlich seit Karl V. die Wahl nur mehr eine Formsache war und in ganz kurzer Zeit beendigt wurde, so scheint es doch früher, zur Zeit des Baues der Kapelle, die Absicht gewesen zu sein, dass, wie bei der Papstwahl die Cardinäle eingemauert worden, auch die Wahlfürsten nicht eher den Wahlort verlassen sollten, bis die Wahl beendigt sei, und diese beiden Oeffnungen zur Darreichung von Lebensmitteln angebracht wurden. Wenig-stens musste jedesmal, auch bei der letzten Wahl noch, während der Zusammen-kunft im Conclave der Reichs-Erbthürhüter den Eingang bewachen.'"

Page 9

Line 32: To you my Lord of Mentz it doth belong,
Having first voice in this Imperial Synod.

This is not the official order of voting. See note regarding ll. 12–13 of p. 5.

Page 10

Line 18: Your Holiness.
See note on l. 7 of p. 5.

Line 36: And to that end *Edward* the Prince of *Wales*.
This is an anachronism. The Edward referred to was the eldest son of Henry III, later Edward I. The first

Notes

Prince of Wales, however, was Edward II. It is in order to state, in this connection, that Edward I was never in Germany and that the romantic adventure attributed to him, in which Hedewick also figures, has no foundation in fact.

Line 37: Hath born his Uncle Company to Germany.
Richard of Cornwall was a younger brother of Henry III.

Page 12

Line 4: the Earl of Leicester.
An allusion to Simon de Montfort.

Line 16: Your Holiness.
See note on l. 7 of p. 5.

Page 13

Line 25: wehrsafflig.
A misprint for *wehrhaftig*, meaning able to carry arms.

Line 26: A man must be a Boy at 40 years.
It is very probable that we have here a reference to the "*Schwabenalter*."

Lines 28-29: Till being soundly box'd about the ears,
His Lord and Master gird him with a sword.

This is an allusion to an old German custom. Elze quotes a parallel passage from *Simplicissimus* (ed. A. Keller, ii, p. 179): "*Dannenhero erhielte ich bald von ihm, dass er mir einen Degen schenckte und mich mit einer Maultasche wehrhaft machte.*"

Page 14

Line 3: Pillars.
See note on l. 2 of p. 7.

Line 25: Holiness.
See note on l. 7 of p. 5.

Page 15

Line 2: Count *Mansfield*.

Elze points out that this name was known to the poet's contemporaries, Count Ernest Mansfield having visited London in the second decade of the 17th century.

Line 33: If we want Venson either red or fallow.

Red and fallow deer were plentiful in England. Fynes Moryson states (*Itinerary*, vol. iv, p. 168), "The Kings Forrests have innumerable heards of Red Deare, and all parts have such plenty of Fallow Deare, as every Gentleman of five hundreth or a thousand pounds rent by the yeere hath a Parke for them inclosed with pales of wood for two or three miles compasse . . . Lastly (without offence be it spoken) I will boldly say, that England (yea perhaps one County thereof) hath more fallow Deare, then all Europe that I have seene." Moryson affirms (vol. iv, p. 139) that in France there were no fallow deer, though there were red deer. In the Netherlands there were no red deer nor had they any enclosed parks for fallow deer. See Moryson (vol. iv, p. 60).

Page 16

Line 1: Wild bore.

The "hunting of wilde boares," says Coryat (*Crudities*, vol. ii, p. 138), "is more exercised by the Germans then by any other Christian nation."

Line 14: lusty.
Merry, like the German *lustig*.

Line 31: your Holiness the Vice.
See note on l. 7 of p. 5.

Line 33: play the Ambodexter.

Regarding the expression "play the Ambodexter," which occurs also in Middleton's *Family of Love*, Act V, sc. 3, Bullen has the following note: "'Play Ambidexter' = keep well with

Notes   87

both sides. A tricksey character in William Bullein's *Dialogue against the Fever Pestilence*, 1564, is named Ambidexter. In legal phraseology the term was applied to 'that juror or embracer that taketh of both parties for the giving of his verdict.'—Cowell's *Interpreter*." Ambidexter, the Vice in Preston's *King Cambises*, thus explains his name:

> "My name is Ambidexter, I signify one
> That with both hands finely can play."

Page 17

Line 2: Take this, and that, and therewithall this Sword.
See note on ll. 28-29 of p. 13.

Line 33: *See dodh, dass ist hier kein gebranch.*
Elze reconstructs this line as follows: *Sieh doch, das ist hier kein gebrauch.*"
Elze cites Shakespeare's *Henry V*, Act V, sc. 2. "*Les dames et demoiselles, pour estre baisées devant leurs noces, il n'est pas la coutume de France.*" Elze refers the reader for information about the English fashion of kissing the ladies to Rye's *England as seen by Foreigners*, 260 *sqq.*

Page 18

Line 16: mock her in her mirth.
The second "her" should, of course, be altered to "your."

Line 28: *Ey Lirbes frawlin nim es all fur gutti.*
Elze changes this passage to "*Ei, liebes Frawlin, nempt es all für gütte.*"

Line 35: *upsy Dutch.*
"'Upsy,'" says Elze, "is printed in black-letter, as if it was a German word.—This is a curious passage, the phrase 'upsy Dutch' having this once no reference to drinking. 'Upsy Dutch' is a corruption either of the Middle Dutch '*op syn dietsch*' or of the Low German '*op syn dütsch.*' It

means 'in his German,' 'in German,' or as the Germans say, '*auf gut Deutsch*,' and, from the language, has been transferred to German manners altogether." In this connection the reference is to the German custom of kissing one's own hand as a form of salutation.

Page 19

Line 10: *filtz geben*.
This phrase signifies to chide. It is an expression, says Elze, that "frequently occurs in the plays of Ayrer, of Duke Heinrich Julius, in *Simplicissimus*, and other writers of the time."

Lines 22 and 31: Prince of *Wales*.
See note on l. 36 of p. 10.

Line 37: *Wass ihr durleichtigkeit dass will dass will mein vattler*.
Elze changes this corrupt passage to "*Was Ihre Durchlauchtigkeit will, das will mein Vater*."

Page 21

Line 30: whore of *Babylon*.
A phrase not infrequently used in the Elizabethan and Jacobean periods. Dekker has a play by this title. Thomas Browne in *Religio Medici*, p. 12, says, speaking of the Pope, "yet can no Ear witness, I ever returned him the Name of Antichrist, Man of Sin, or Whore of Babylon."

Page 22

Line 21: *Pontificalibus*.
The following explanation of this word appears in Murray's *New English Dictionary*: "Lat., abl. of pontificālia (The vestments and other insignia of a bishop). Almost always used in the phrase *in his* (or *their*) *pontificalibus*, in imitation of the Latin phrase. Hence (sometimes) improperly as if an ordinary English noun."

Notes

Page 23

Line 17: griping at our lots.
Elze calls attention to the fact that the dramatist has discarded the more usual phrase, "drawing our lots," to adopt a phrase that reads like a translation of the German idiom *beim Greifen nach den Loosen*.

Line 37: By Letters which I'l strew within the Wood.
See Introduction.

Page 24

Line 5: To rid my foes.
Elze compares this construction of the verb "to rid" to the line in *Richard II*, Act V, sc. 4, "I am the king's friend and will rid his foe."

Line 17: To Revel it with Rhadamant in Hell.
Rhadamant was a judge of the Nether World. A Stygian vocabulary was characteristic of the plays of Seneca, which exerted considerable influence upon the Elizabethan drama.

Line 20: plumper Bowr.
Elze interprets this phrase as "a lubberly peasant."

Page 25

Line 8: Till thou in *Aix* be Crowned Emperour.
Aix = Aix-la-Chapelle.
According to Fynes Moryson (*Itinerary*, vol. iv, p. 261), "the Emperour was to be chosen at Franckfort, crowned at Aix-la-Chapelle, and was, unless prevented by some lawful impediment, to hold his first Court in Nurnberg."

Stage direction: *Enter two Bowrs*.
As Prof. Parrott points out (*Anglia*, vol. xxx, Neue Folge, 18, p. 361), this is an anticipation of the entrance of Hans and Jerick four lines later. It should be omitted.

90 Alphonsus

Stage direction: Jerick *reads.*
This stage direction should follow the words in the next line "*Hear weiter.*"

Lines 28–29: *versahmen.*
Should read "*versäumen.*"

Line 30: Karl.
Should read Kerl, as Elze points out.

Page 26

Line 6: *jenner selleuch.*
"*jener soll euch*" is Elze's substitution.

Line 7: *bried.*
Should read "*berürt,*" according to Elze.

Line 20: *Dat dich potts velten leiden.*
Elze translates this "may the falling sickness hurt you" and compares the phrase with "*Dass Dich Potz Veltes marter schend*" [Ayrer's *Dramas* (ed. Keller, iv, 2816)], and "*Dass dich sant Veltin schend*" (*Ibid.* v, 3216).

Line 23: *harr ich will dich lernen.*
Elze compares this to the line in Ayrer's *Dramas* (ed. Keller, iv, 2695): "*Harr! ich will dich bringn von der Gassn.*"

Page 27

Lines 3–4: *So mus ich meren.*
Elze emends to "*so muss ich mich wehren.*"

Line 6: *karle.*
See p. 25, l. 30.

Lines 24–26: how dare you then
Being Princes offer to lay hands on me?
That is the Hangmans Office here in Dutch-land.

Notes 91

"The Germans," says Fynes Moryson (*Itinerary*, vol. iv, p. 287), "hold it reprochfull to apprehend any malefactor, which is onely done by the Serjeants of the Hangmans disgracefull Family."

Page 29

Line 10: wait up.
Elze points out that this is a literal translation of *aufwarten*.

Page 30

Line 9: upsie Dutch.
See note on l. 35 of p. 18.

Page 31

Lines 1–2: In Saxon Land you know it is the use,
That the first night the Bridegroom spares the Bride.

Regarding the custom here alluded to, Elze has the following note: "It was a far-spread custom in the early Christian church for newly-married couples to pass the first three nights in prayer, according to the pious example set by Toby (Book of Toby, ch. 8); by such continence they hoped to propitiate heaven and to call down the blessings of God on their marriage. This custom was expressly enjoined by a council held at Carthage in 398, and particularly prevailed in Italy and in France. From the information we can gather on the subject, it appears highly improbable that the Germans should ever have shown the same implicit obedience to this mandate of the church as their western and southern neighbours. Their cooler blood did not require such a check to their desires; they rather took a legal view of matrimony and, according to the Saxon law, did not think it consummated before the young couple had been covered by one blanket. It therefore formed part of the marriage ceremonies almost down to the end of the 16th century, that the young couple, in presence of the witnesses and guests, and without undressing, ascended a couch and there for a little while lay down under the same cover."

Line 22: *dis nicht ben mee.*
Elze changes to "*dis nacht bey me.*"

Line 24: *mist begeran.*
Elze substitutes "*nicht begeren.*"

Line 28: a *Jacobs* staff.
An astronomical instrument.

Page 32

Line 1: We drink about.
Regarding this custom Fynes Moryson (*Itinerary*, vol. iv, pp. 37–38) says: "For equality they [Germans] drinke round, especially in Saxony, except in curtesie they sometimes drinke out of course to a Guest; and this equall manner of drinking, they say had its first originall from a pleasant or rather wicked Act, of an undutifull Sonne, who receiving a boxe of the eare from his Father, and daring not strike him againe, did notwithstanding strike his next Neighbour as hard a blow as hee received, desiring him to passe it round about the Table as a frolicke, in these wordes: Lasset umb gehen, so kriagt der vatter auch was; Let it goe round, so my Father shall have it in his course, and so more modestly or lesse wickedly hee revenged himselfe. While all drinke in this manner circularly out of one and the same pot, they scoffe at him that drinkes the last remainder saying proverbially that hee shall marry an old trot."

Page 33

Stage direction at head of page: *with a gamon of raw bacon, and links or puddings in a platter.*
The "*links or puddings*" were sausages.

Notes 93

Fynes Moryson (*Itinerary*, vol. iv, p. 24) says that "in lower Germany they supply the meale with *bacon* and great dried *puddings*, which puddings are savory and so pleasant, as in their kind of mirth they wish proverbially for Kurtz predigen, lange worsten, that is; Short sermons and long puddings." See also Fynes Moryson (*Itinerary*, vol. i, p. 27) where "raw bacon" and "dried puddings" are mentioned in conjunction.

Stage direction: a Miter.
See note on l. 24 of p. 43.

Stage direction at head of page: *Corances*.
Corances were garlands. See note on l. 38 of p. 60.

Line 8: dorp.
dorp = village (German *dorf*).
Stanyhurst uses this word in his translation of *Æneid*, Bk. I, "where dorps and cottages earst stood."

Line 12: nippitate.
The meaning of this word is strong, good, prime. In Murray's *New English Dictionary* instances of its use in connection with liquors of various kinds are given. *Weakest goeth to the Wall:* "Fresh ale, prime ale, nappie ale, nippitate ale!" *Look about You:* "two bottles of nippitate sack."

Line 15: *spell*.
Should be *spiel* according to Elze.

Line 15: *Rommer daunteu*.
Should be *rommer dantzen*. "*Rommer* or *rummer* is a corruption of *herum*" (Elze).

Line 20: an upspring.
This, according to Elze, was the *Hüpfauf*, "the last and consequently wildest dance at the old German merrymakings." Elze refers to Ayrer's *Dramas* (ed. Keller, iv, 2840 and 2846):

> "*Ey, jtzt geht erst der hupffauff an.*
> *Ey, Herr, jtzt kummt erst der hupffauff.*"

Stage direction at bottom of page: *fore dance.*
A literal translation of the German *Vortanz.*

Line 27: *leffel morgen.*
To be translated "make love to-morrow," the verb *leffeln* or *löffeln* meaning "to make love." Elze says "*löffeln* frequently occurs in the German writers of the time."

Line 27: when thou com'st to house.
"To house" suggests the German phrase *nach Hause.*

Page 34

Line 2: *Skelt bowre.*
Elze changes to "*'Sgelt, bowr.*"

Line 5: *fcenudt.*
Elze suggests "*freundt.*"

Line 5: *frolocken.*
Elze changes to "*fröhlichen.*"

Lines 7–8: Half this I drink unto your Highness health,
  It is the first since we were joynd in Office.

Coryat says (*Crudities,* vol. ii, p. 174): "It is their [the Germans'] custome whensoever they drink to another, to see their glasse filled up incontinent, (for therein they most commonly drinke) and then they deliver it into the hand of him to whome they drinke, esteeming him a very curteous man that doth pledge the whole, according to the old verse:

'*Germanus mihi frater eris si pocula siccas.*'"

Line 22: Spanish flies.
A reference to the drug cantharides.

Notes

Page 36

Line 3: untrust my points.
That is, untied the points that joined the breeches to the doublet.

Line 31: so foul a fact.
Possibly "fact" should read act, as Elze suggests, though not necessarily so. There is a similar use of the word in the sense of deed in *Tamburlaine*, Part I, Act III, sc. 2: " Will rattle forth his facts of war and blood."

Page 37

Line 9: With *Saxon* lansknights.
"Their [the Germans'] Footemen," says Moryson (*Itinerary*, vol. iv, p. 274), "are vulgarly called Lantzknechten, that is, Servants with Lances, and the best of them are those of Tyroll, Suevia, and Westphalia. Commonly they are corpulent, and of a dull or lesse fiery spirit, yet are of great strength in fighting a battell, by reason of their strong members, and the constant order they use in fighting. And they are armed with Lances most fit for their strength, rather than with Calivers, requiring nimblenesse in charging and discharging."

Line 9: *Switzers*.
The mercenary troops of Switzerland.

Stage direction: *Enter* Alphonsus,
and
Lines 28–32.
Prof. Parrott has an ingenious solution for the difficulties that present themselves in these lines when taken in conjunction with the later text. He assigns lines 28–29 to Alexander, postponing Alphonsus' entrance until just before line 30. His arrangement reads thus:

Exeunt.

[*Alex coming forward.*] This dangerous plot was happily
overheard.
Here didst thou listen in a blessed
hour.

Enter Alphonsus.

[*Alp.*] Alexander, where dost thou hide thyself?
I've sought thee, etc.

Page 38

Line 11: The Prince of *Wales.*
See note on l. 36 of p. 10.

Line 25: I am fond.
fond = foolish.

Line 35: By night all Cats are gray.
Elze speaks of this as "a German proverb," which, he thinks, "will nowhere else be found in English." This statement is altogether too sweeping. Prof. Thomas Parrott, in his scholarly edition of Chapman's Tragedies, points out that in John Heywood's *Proverbs*, 1562, Part I, chap. v, occurs the sentence, "When all candles be out, all cats be gray." To this might be added that another variant of the same proverb appears in Shelton's translation of *Don Quixote* (1612–20): "If your highness has no mind that the government you promised should be given me, God made me of less, and perhaps it may be easier for Sancho, the Squire, to get to Heaven than for Sancho, the Governor. *In the dark all cats are gray.*"

Line 36: Prince of *Wales.*
See note on l. 36 of p. 10.

Page 39

Line 1: And fild thy beating vains with stealing joy.
Robertson calls attention to the close parallel between

Notes

this line and the one in Peele's *Arraignment of Paris*, Act II, sc. 1, l. 176: "To ravish all thy beating veins with joy."

Page 40

Line 3: travants.
"The word 'travant' seems again to be borrowed from the German" (Elze).

Stage direction: *trayls the Empress by the hair*.
A not uncommon situation in the drama. In *Bussy D'Ambois*, Act V, sc. 1, the stage direction reads: "Enter Montsurry bare, unbrac't, pulling Tamyra in by the haire." In *Robert Earl of Huntington*, Part II, Matilda is led by the hair by two soldiers.

Lines 19–20: Hast thou in secret *Clytemnestra* like
Hid thy Ægestus thy adulterous love.

Clytemnestra, the wife of Agamemnon, had during her husband's absence committed adultery with Ægisthus, son of Thyestes. With her paramour she planned the destruction of Agamemnon. Although Cassandra warned the King, her prophecy was as usual not heeded. So it happened that while Agamemnon was bathing, shortly before the banquet which was to be given in honour of his return, he was murdered.

Page 41

Line 3: Kennels.
The surface drain of a street; the gutter.

Line 4: And cut the Nose from thy bewitching face.
See Introduction.

Page 42

Line 3: hurley burley.
In *The Garden of Eloquence*, 1577, by Henry Peacham, is

found the following definition: "Onomatopeia, when we invent, devise, fayne, and make a name intimating the sownd of that it signifyeth, as *hurly burly*, for an uprore and tumultuous stirre."

Page 43

Line 19: rocket.
A misprint for rochet, a vestment of linen, worn usually by bishops and abbots, and resembling a surplice.

Line 24: Instead of Miter, and a Crossier Staff.
Coryat in his *Crudities* (vol. i, p. 177) describes these two articles as worn and carried by the Bishop of Paris: "He himselfe was that day in his sumptuous Pontificalities, wearing religious ornaments of great price, like a second Aaron, with his Episcopall staffe in his hand, bending round at the toppe, called by us English men a Croisier, and his Miter on his head of cloth of silver, with two long labels hanging downe behind his neck."
Murray's *New English Dictionary* gives the following explanation of the crosier: "In the 16th century *crosier's* or *crosier-staff* was a common term for the episcopal crook, borne by the *crociarius*, and at length the crook itself was called the *crosier*. Many 19th century ecclesiastical antiquaries have erroneously transferred the name to the cross borne before an archbishop."

Page 45

Line 1: in the fact was slain.
See note on l. 31 of p. 36.

Line 7: Holiness.
See note on l. 7 of p. 5.

Lines 27–32.
These lines are so garbled that their proper form must be given to make them intelligible.

Notes 99

Sast dorh licbes doister should read *Sag doch, liebe dochter*.
dicselbir-maft is intended for *dieselbe nacht*.

Ich ha mist audes gemeint should be restored to *Ich hab nicht anders gemeint*.

allrin gesiflaffne is a typographical blunder for *allein geschlaffen*.

bundt sislaffet all but effectually disguises the words *undt schlaffet*.

The corrected readings are taken from Elze.

Page 46

Line 13: *satt mist*.
Should read *hatt nicht* (Elze).

Line 14: *zum sagun*.
Elze reconstructs to read **zu sagen**.

Line 15: *gerfralet*.
Elze changes to *gefület*.

Line 21: *I leff—snlt*
Elze substitutes *Ey lef—solt*.

Line 36: Prince of *Wales*.
See note on l. 36 of p. 10.

Page 49

Stage direction at head of page: (*carried in the Couch*).
Albright makes the statement (*The Shaksperian Stage*, p. 144) that "the carrying of a couch from one room to another, or moving it around in the same room, seems to have been a very conventional thing. For example, in *The Roman Actor*, V, 1, Cæsar calls out, 'Bring my Couch there: *Enter with Couch*. A sudden but a secure Drowsiness invites me to repose myself.'" Among the instances cited by Albright (p. 145) of the carrying in of people on articles of furniture are the following:—"*Gentleman Usher*, V, 1. 'Enter Strozza, Vincentio, brought in a chaire,

Benevenius, Pogio, Cynanche, with a guard, Strozza before & Medice.' . . . *King Lear* (folio, 1623), IV, 7. 'Enter Lear in a chaire carried by Servants.'"

Line 7: cold Tartarian hills.
Robertson recalls the phrase in *Tamburlaine*, Part I, Act III, sc. 3, l. 151: "white Tartarian hills."

Lines 8–10: I feel th' ascending flame lick up my blood,
Mine Entrals shrink together like a scrowl
Of burning parchment, and my Marrow fries.

Koeppel remarks (*Quellen Studien zu den Dramen George Chapman's, Philip Massinger's und John Ford's*, p. 79) that he is in accord with Elze in finding an echo of Shakespeare in the mendacious utterances of Alphonsus when the Emperor pretends he is suffering from the effects of poison. The latter employs about the same figures of speech as does King John when poisoned.

"K. John. There is so hot a summer in my bosom,
That all my bowels crumble up to dust:
I am a scribbled form, drawn with a pen
Upon a parchment, and against this fire
Do I shrink up." (V, 7, 30 ff.)

Line 10: my Marrow fries.
The susceptibility of the marrow to the influence of heat, whether actually or figuratively, constitutes a favourite allusion in the literature of the time. Compare with Stanyhurst's translation of the *Æneid*, Bk. IV:

"whilst deepelye the flamd fire
Kindleth in her marrow,"

and *Bussy D'Ambois*, Act IV, sc. 2, l. 189:

"like lightning melt
The very marrow."

Notes

Line 29: cold swift running *Rhyn*.

Elze remarks that "the Rhine could hardly be better characterised in so few words than by the mention of its two pre-eminent features."

Line 37: holiness.
See note on l. 7 of p. 5.

Page 50

Line 14: fondly.
In the sense of foolishly.

Page 51

Line 25: His holiness.
See note on l. 7 of p. 5.

Line 34: Bed-role of the Saints.

Bed-role or bead-roll—"a list of persons to be specially prayed for. Obs. or arch." (Murray's *New English Dictionary*).

Page 52

Line 28: fond.
See note on l. 25 of p. 38 and note on l. 14 of p. 50.

Line 32: Come forth thou perfect map of miserie.

The word map in the sense of picture or image occurs frequently in the drama of the period. *Richard II*, Act V, sc. 1, "Thou map of honour"; *Gentleman Usher*, Act I, "a map of basenesse"; Marlowe's *Dido*, Act I, sc. 1, "the map of weather-beaten woe"; *Titus Andronicus*, Act III, sc. 2, "Thou map of woe," etc.

Page 53

Line 8: *Edward of Wales*.
See note on l. 36 of p. 10.

Page 54

Line 18: Athamas.
Ino, the wife of Athamas, incurred the wrath of Hera, because she had given suck to the infant Bacchus. As a punishment she was pursued by her raving husband and with her youngest son, Melicertes, hurled by him into the sea.

Line 21: Then like *Virginius* will I kill my Child.
An allusion to the slaying of Virginia by her father.

Line 27: *Ah myne seete Edouart.*
Should read *Ach mein süsse Eduart* (Elze).

Line 29: *friendlich one.*
This is a misspelling of *freindlich an* (Elze).
seete hart = sweetheart.

Page 58

Line 34: Shall fasten him in fetters to the Chair.
A stock situation that occurs in *Antonio's Revenge*, Act V, sc. 2, *The Woman Hater*, Act V, sc. 5, and other plays.

Page 60

Line 38: rose Corance.
Elze notes that "in Germany a 'Rosenkranz' served as a symbol of virginity, and therefore in old popular songs often denotes maidenhead itself."

In connection with this passage and the use of "corances" in the stage direction that appears on the top of p. 33, a little further explanation of the rose corance seems in order. The German custom of wearing garlands on the head is described at length by Fynes Moryson (*Itinerary*, vol. iv, 209–210): "Citizens daughters and Virgines of inferiour sort, weare nothing upon their heads, but their haire woven with laces, and so gathered on the fore-part of the head, with the forehead stroked up plaine, and upon the fore-part of the head the Gentlewomen weare a border of pearle, and all other from the highest to the lowest, commonly weare garlands of roses, (which they call Crantzes).

"For they keepe Roses all Winter in little pots of earth, whereof they open one each saturday at night, and distribute the Roses among the women of the house, to the very kitchin maide; others keepe them all in one pot, and weekely take as many Roses as they neede, and cover the rest, keeping them fresh till the next Summer. And the common sort mingle guilded nutmegs with these Roses, and make garlands thereof: Only women weare these Garlands in Winter, but in Summer time men of the better sort weare them within doores, and men of the common sort weare them going abroade. They keepe Roses all Winter in this sort, they choose the closest and thickest buds of all kinds of Roses but the Damaske Roses best keepe the smell, and other kindes the colour. Then they take a pot of earth, and sprinckle some bay salt in the bottome, and lay these buds severally, not very close one to the other, in two rowes one above the other, which done they sprinckle the same, and wet all the buds with two little glasses of Rhenish Wine, and againe sprinckle them with bay salt in greater quantity, yet such as it may not eate the leaves. In like sort they put up each two rowes of buds, till the pot be full, which they cover with wood or leade, so as no aire can enter, and then lay it up in a cold cellar, where no sunne comes. When they take out the buds, they dip them in luke warme water, or put them into the Oven when the bread is taken out, which makes the leaves open with the turning of the buds betweene two fingers, then they dip a feather in rhenish wine, and wipe the leaves therewith, to refresh the colour, and some doe the like with rose water, to renew the smell."

Page 63

Line 34: Caius Cassius.
Cassius, after his defeat at Philippi, believing all was lost, compelled Pindarus, his freedman, to put him to death.

Page 64

Line 11: Thou knewst too much of me to live with me.
See Introduction.

Line 22: I crave thy Highness leave to bind thee first.
See note on l. 34 of p. 58.

Page 65

Lines 38–40: *Alphonsus* doth renounce the joyes of Heaven,
The sight of Angells and his Saviours blood,
And gives his Soul unto the Devills power.

This renunciation is hardly less sweeping than that of Marlowe's *Faustus* (sc. VI):

"And Faustus vows never to look to Heaven,
Never to name God, or to pray to him,
To burn his Scriptures, slay his ministers,
And make my spirits pull his churches down."

Page 67

Line 3: *Thetis* Son.
Achilles.

Line 3: *Menetiades*.
Patroclus.

Lines 14–15: This happy hand, blest be my hand therefore,
Reveng'd my Fathers death upon his soul.

See Introduction.

Line 37: broken on the Wheel.
See Introduction.

Page 69

Line 10: More furiously than ere Laocoon ran.

Notes

See *Æneid*, Bk. II, 1. 41: *Laocoon ardens summa decurrit ab arce.*

Line 11: *Troy's* overthrow.
A reference to the wooden horse, which the Trojans admitted within their walls.

Line 28: What Bull of *Phalaris*.
In this contrivance, a brazen bull, objectionable persons were slowly roasted to death. According to Jebb (*Life of Richard Bentley*) "as early as 500 B.C. Phalaris' name had become a proverb for horrible cruelty, not only in Sicily, but throughout Hellas."

In Fletcher's *Valentinian*, Act V, sc. 2, there is allusion to the torturing device cited above: "The brazen bull of Phalaris was feign'd."

Page 70

Lines 2–3: There let the Judas, on a Jewish Gallowes,
  Hang by the heels between two English Mastives.

See Introduction.

Line 18: *Aix.*
See note on 1. 8 of p. 25.

www.ingramcontent.com/pod-product-compliance
Lightning Source LLC
LaVergne TN
LVHW011203080426
835508LV00007B/570